Cleopatra's Final Secret:

Kathleen Martinez's Historic Collaboration with Titanic Explorer Bob Ballard

Myrl Langston

Copyright page

Disclaimer page

This book is written for educational and informational purposes only. The content is based on publicly available information, archaeological reports, documentary sources, historical records, and research materials available at the time of publication.

This work is not officially endorsed, sponsored, or approved by Dr. Kathleen Martinez, Dr. Robert Ballard, National Geographic, the Egyptian Ministry of Tourism and Antiquities, or any other individuals, organizations, or institutions mentioned herein. Any opinions, interpretations, or conclusions drawn are those of the author and do not necessarily reflect the views of the aforementioned parties.

While every effort has been made to ensure the accuracy of the archaeological information presented, the field of archaeology is constantly evolving. New discoveries, research methodologies, and interpretations may emerge that could modify or contradict information contained in this book. Readers are encouraged to consult current archaeological publications and official sources for the most up-to-date findings.

The search for Cleopatra's tomb and related archaeological investigations described in this book represent ongoing research projects. Conclusions presented should be understood as working theories and hypotheses that may be subject to revision based on future discoveries and analysis.

The author acknowledges the groundbreaking work of Dr. Kathleen Martinez and Dr. Robert Ballard in their respective fields and presents this account as a tribute to their contributions to archaeological and oceanographic exploration.

Table of Contents

The Most Ambitious Underwater Archaeological Expedition Of Our Time

Twenty-three earthquakes. That's what changed everything.

Between 320 and 1303 AD, the Mediterranean coast of Egypt shuddered and cracked as seismic waves rippled through the ancient world. With each tremor, with each tsunami that followed, more of Egypt's coastal treasures slipped beneath the waves. Among them, potentially, lay the greatest archaeological prize of all time: the tomb of Cleopatra VII, the last pharaoh of Egypt.

For over two millennia, this mystery has haunted historians, archaeologists, and treasure hunters alike. Where did the most powerful woman of the ancient world choose to spend eternity? The question seemed destined to remain unanswered until a Dominican criminal lawyer named Kathleen Martinez decided she could solve what others could not. Her audacious theory would eventually lead her to partner with Bob Ballard, the legendary oceanographer who found the Titanic resting in the Atlantic's depths. What unfolded in the waters off Taposiris Magna in 2024 represents something unprecedented in the annals of archaeology. Never before have two such different worlds of exploration merged with such dramatic results. On one side stood Martinez, a woman who traded her legal career for twenty years of relentless digging in the Egyptian desert, driven by an unshakeable belief that everyone else was looking in the wrong place. On the other stood Ballard, the man whose deep-sea robots had revolutionized our understanding of what lies beneath the ocean's surface.

Their collaboration began with a simple but extraordinary question: What if Cleopatra's tomb wasn't lost to time, but to water?

The answer came in September 2025, when their joint expedition revealed "massive man-made structures off the coast of Taposiris Magna," structures that had remained hidden beneath Mediterranean waters for nearly two thousand years. The discovery sent shockwaves through the archaeological community and captured global attention in a way that few expeditions ever do. The story of how this partnership came to be is itself remarkable. Martinez, who had spent two decades meticulously excavating the Taposiris Magna temple complex west of Alexandria, had discovered something that made her reconsider everything she thought she knew about Cleopatra's final resting place. A tunnel, pointing directly toward the sea. For most archaeologists, water represents the end of the trail. For Martinez, it represented a new beginning.

Her decision to reach out to Ballard was born from desperation and inspiration in equal measure. Here was a man who had spent his career finding the impossible in the deepest, darkest places on Earth. If anyone could help her follow Cleopatra's trail beneath the waves, it would be the explorer who had given the world its first glimpse of the

Titanic since 1912. Ballard's response was immediate and enthusiastic. The prospect of applying his cutting-edge underwater technology to one of history's greatest unsolved mysteries appealed to every fiber of his explorer's soul. More than that, he recognized something in Martinez that spoke to his own experiences of being dismissed by establishment figures who couldn't see beyond conventional wisdom.

What makes their collaboration so extraordinary isn't just the technology they brought to bear on the problem, or even the stunning discoveries they made. It's the fusion of two fundamentally different approaches to exploration. Martinez approaches archaeology like the criminal lawyer she once was, treating ancient history as a cold case to be cracked through careful analysis of evidence. Ballard brings the systematic methodology of deep-sea exploration, where precision and technology must overcome the hostile environment of the ocean depths. Their joint expedition revealed structures over 20 feet high, including polished floors, cemented blocks, towering columns, and multiple ancient anchors, all dating to Cleopatra's era. But perhaps more significant than any individual discovery was what they proved possible. For the first time in archaeological history, land-based excavation and deep-sea exploration had been seamlessly integrated into a single, coordinated search effort.

The stakes could hardly be higher. Cleopatra VII wasn't just another ancient ruler. She was a polyglot who spoke nine languages, a shrewd political strategist who maintained Egypt's independence for nearly two decades, and a woman whose intelligence and charisma made her one of the most influential figures of her age. Finding her tomb wouldn't just solve an archaeological mystery; it would potentially rewrite our understanding of the Ptolemaic dynasty and the final chapter of pharaonic Egypt. Martinez had already spent twenty years building the case for her theory. Her team had discovered hundreds of coins depicting Cleopatra VII throughout the Taposiris Magna site, including more than 330 coins found hidden in what she calls a "sacred trench" near the temple wall. They had uncovered gilded mummies, evidence of elite burials from Cleopatra's time, and artifacts that painted a compelling picture of the temple's importance during the queen's reign.

But it was the discovery of that tunnel, leading from the temple directly toward the Mediterranean, that changed everything. Martinez realized that if parts of the ancient complex had been submerged by centuries of seismic activity, then perhaps Cleopatra's tomb lay not in some undiscovered chamber beneath the desert, but in the underwater ruins of what had once been a magnificent coastal sanctuary. The technology Ballard brought to this quest represents the cutting edge of underwater exploration. His team created detailed sonar maps covering nearly six miles of underwater terrain, identifying specific targets for diving operations. The structures they found, dubbed "Salam 5" and "Three Sisters," included rectangular stone constructions reminiscent of the broken statue pedestals found at the Taposiris Magna temple above water.

For Ballard, this expedition represents a return to the kind of exploration that first made his reputation. Long before he became famous for finding the Titanic, he was discovering new forms of life around hydrothermal vents and pushing the boundaries of what was possible in the deep ocean. The search for Cleopatra's tomb combines his love of technological innovation with the thrill of historical discovery.

The emotional weight of their collaboration is impossible to ignore. Martinez speaks with the passion of someone who has staked her entire career on a single, seemingly impossible theory. "Nobody can tell me that Cleopatra is not at Taposiris Magna," she declares with the conviction that has driven her through twenty years of skepticism from the archaeological establishment. Her determination is matched by Ballard's infectious enthusiasm for discovery. Upon seeing the first images from their underwater survey, he couldn't contain his excitement: "There is an island with a harbor that has a tunnel leading from the temple, we think, to that very spot. This doesn't get any better." Their story has captured global attention not just because of what they might find, but because of what they represent. In an age of specialization, where academic disciplines often operate in isolation, Martinez and Ballard demonstrate the power of cross-disciplinary collaboration. Their partnership proves that sometimes the most important breakthroughs come not from looking deeper into what we already know, but from looking sideways into unexplored possibilities.

As Martinez puts it with characteristic determination: "I'm not going to stop. For me, it's a matter of time." Whether they ultimately find Cleopatra's tomb or not, their collaboration has already achieved something remarkable. They have shown that the most ambitious archaeological expeditions of our time require not just courage and persistence, but the willingness to venture beyond the boundaries of conventional exploration.

The waters off Taposiris Magna now hold secrets that have been hidden for two millennia. Thanks to the unprecedented partnership between a determined Dominican archaeologist and America's most famous deep-sea explorer, we are closer than ever to unlocking the final mystery of ancient Egypt's most legendary queen.

Chapter 1: The Dreamer From Santo Domingo

The humid air of Santo Domingo carried the scent of old paper and leather bindings on the afternoon Kathleen Teresa Martinez Berry drew her first breath in 1966. She entered a world where knowledge wasn't just valued—it was sacred. Her father, Professor Fausto Martinez, wasn't simply a legal scholar; he was the keeper of the Caribbean's most extraordinary treasure: the largest private library in the region. Within those walls, shelves stretched from floor to ceiling, holding volumes that had sailed across oceans to find their home in this corner of the Dominican Republic.

From the moment she could toddle across the polished floors, little Kathleen understood that this wasn't just a house—it was a temple of learning. Her father treated books with the reverence others reserved for religious artifacts, and young Kathleen absorbed this devotion through every fiber of her being. The child who would one day challenge centuries of archaeological wisdom was already showing signs of her restless intellect.

At five years old, most children were content with crayons and coloring books. Not Kathleen. On her first day of preschool, when handed drawing materials, she politely raised her tiny hand. "I can draw at home," she informed the startled teacher. "Is there anything you can teach me?" The boldness in that small voice would echo through the decades ahead, propelling her toward discoveries that would astonish the world.

Her mother, of Franco-English descent, watched with knowing eyes as their daughter devoured book after book with an appetite that seemed impossible to satisfy. But it was Professor Fausto who truly understood the mind blossoming before them. Every week, he would select new volumes from his collection, presenting them to Kathleen like carefully chosen gifts. The ritual never varied: after she finished reading, father and daughter would sit in his study, surrounded by thousands of volumes, and discuss what she had learned.

These weren't casual conversations. They were intellectual sparring matches that would have challenged graduate students. The country's most prominent thinkers gathered every Sunday in the Martinez home for her father's legendary salons. While other children played outside, Kathleen was often allowed to sit quietly in the corner, listening as politicians, philosophers, and scholars debated the great questions of their time. She absorbed their passionate arguments, their careful reasoning, their willingness to challenge accepted truths.

The little girl thrived in this rarefied atmosphere. She skipped grades with startling regularity, her teachers marveling at a mind that seemed to operate on a different frequency entirely. But it wasn't just academics that captured her attention. Kathleen channeled her competitive spirit into chess, becoming a champion. She mastered swimming, threw herself into judo and karate, and conquered the piano with the same intensity she brought to everything else.

Yet even surrounded by all this intellectual stimulation, one subject captured her imagination above all others: ancient Egypt. At the tender age of five, while other children were fascinated by fairy tales, Kathleen found herself drawn to the mysteries of pharaohs and pyramids. Her father's library contained extensive collections on Egyptian history, and she would spend hours poring over texts about hieroglyphs, mummies, and the legendary queens who ruled the Nile.

Her fascination wasn't casual. Even as a child, Kathleen approached ancient Egypt with the methodical curiosity that would later make her a formidable archaeologist. She studied maps of temple sites, memorized the names of dynasties, and became particularly captivated by stories of Egypt's last pharaoh—a brilliant queen named Cleopatra VII who had ruled the most powerful nation on earth.

The seeds of obsession were already taking root. When Kathleen declared at fifteen that she wanted to become an archaeologist and work in Egypt, her parents exchanged worried glances. They had created a monster of intellect, but they also lived in the practical world of the Dominican Republic in the 1980s. Archaeology was a luxury for wealthy American and European universities. For a girl from Santo Domingo, no matter how brilliant, such dreams seemed impossibly far-fetched.

"You'll never have a serious job," her father told her gently but firmly. "You can't make a living from that profession." The words stung, but they also planted something else—a determination that would burn quietly for years, waiting for the right moment to burst into flame.

The Reluctant Lawyer (1984-2004)

The transformation happened with stunning swiftness. The dreamy child who had spent her afternoons lost in tales of Egyptian queens became a legal prodigy who graduated law school at eighteen. Even in the Dominican Republic, where students often entered university younger than their American counterparts, this was extraordinary. Kathleen hadn't just completed her degree—she had conquered it with the same relentless drive she brought to everything else.

The Dominican legal system demanded more than theoretical knowledge. Law students were required to try actual cases before graduation, and this was where Kathleen truly proved herself. While her classmates nervously stumbled through their first courtroom appearances, she took on a case that made veteran attorneys step back in amazement. A prominent banker had been framed in a politically charged scandal, and no established lawyer in the country wanted to touch it. The risks were too high, the political implications too dangerous. Kathleen saw opportunity where others saw peril. She threw herself into the case with forensic intensity, treating it like an archaeological dig. She excavated evidence, uncovered witness testimony, and built her argument with the patience of someone searching for ancient artifacts. When the verdict came down—not guilty—the legal community took notice. The city's most prominent criminal attorney approached her with an offer that would have made law school graduates twice her age weep with envy.

"Now, I will teach you the law," he told her, recognizing raw talent that could be molded into something extraordinary.

For the next twenty years, Kathleen built a reputation that stretched far beyond Santo Domingo. She became one of the Dominican Republic's most sought-after criminal defense attorneys, the kind of lawyer wealthy clients fought to retain and prosecutors respected even as they opposed her in court. Her cases were often politically charged, frequently dangerous, and always meticulously prepared. She developed a client base that would remain loyal for decades, drawn not just to her legal brilliance but to her fearless approach to justice. But success came at a price. The young woman who had once dreamed of excavating ancient tombs found herself buried instead in legal briefs and court filings. The intellectual challenges were real—each case was a puzzle to solve, each client a human story to understand—but something essential was missing. Late at night, when the law books were closed and the house was quiet, Kathleen found her mind wandering to those childhood dreams of desert sands and hidden treasures.

Marriage brought new complications and opportunities. When her husband decided to pursue cardiology studies in Madrid,

Kathleen saw a chance for adventure. Spain represented possibility, a break from the routine that had come to define her life in Santo Domingo. They packed up their lives and moved to a country where flamenco music drifted through narrow streets and centuries-old architecture whispered stories of conquest and glory. But Madrid also brought unexpected challenges. For a woman accustomed to the intellectual intensity of courtroom battles, staying home with a newborn felt like exile. Kathleen had never been someone who could sit idle, and motherhood, beautiful as it was, left her restless in ways she hadn't anticipated. Her mind, trained for complex problems and high-stakes decisions, craved stimulation beyond diaper changes and feeding schedules.

The solution came to her during one of those long nights when her infant daughter refused to sleep. If she was going to be awake anyway, why not use the time productively? She enrolled in a master's program in finance, attacking the coursework with the same intensity she had once brought to criminal cases. Mathematics and market analysis became her new puzzles to solve, spreadsheets and economic theories her new battlegrounds. When their second child arrived, the pattern repeated itself. But this time, Kathleen made a different choice. Instead of another practical degree, she finally allowed herself to follow the dream that had never truly died. She enrolled in an archaeology program, and suddenly the world shifted back into focus.

The Awakening: From Finance to Archaeology (1999-2004)

The moment of reckoning came not in a classroom or library, but in the familiar comfort of her father's study back in Santo Domingo. Kathleen was browsing through the shelves that had shaped her childhood, looking for something to read during a brief visit home. Her fingers traced the spines of countless volumes before settling on a worn copy of Shakespeare's "Antony and Cleopatra."

She pulled it from the shelf, and her father glanced up from his desk with a dismissive wave.

"Don't waste your time with that," Professor Fausto said, his voice carrying the authority that had intimidated scholars for decades. "Cleopatra was nothing more than a political schemer. She's not even worthy of a historical footnote."

The words hit Kathleen like a physical blow. Here was her father—the man who had taught her to question everything, to dig deeper, to never accept surface explanations—dismissing one of history's most fascinating figures without evidence or investigation. The daughter who had learned to argue cases in courtrooms found her voice in that dusty study.

"Why do you speak of the queen like this?" she demanded, her legal training kicking in. "How do you know? What are your sources?"

The challenge hung in the air between them. Professor Fausto looked up, perhaps seeing for the first time that his daughter had grown into a woman capable of intellectual combat. But instead of backing down or providing evidence, he simply shrugged. Ancient history wasn't his specialty. He was simply repeating what everyone had always said about Cleopatra.

That night, Kathleen made a vow that would reshape the rest of her life: she would find out the truth for herself.

The promise seemed simple enough, but the reality was daunting. This was 1990, in a small Caribbean island nation where the internet didn't exist and archaeological resources were scarce. Kathleen approached the challenge like the criminal attorney she was, treating Cleopatra's story as a cold case that had been closed prematurely. She read everything she could find—Plutarch, Plato, Socrates, and especially the Roman historians who had shaped Cleopatra's reputation for two millennia.

What she discovered infuriated her. "History is written by the winners," she realized, and the Romans had certainly won their war against Egypt. They had systematically destroyed Cleopatra's image, reducing a brilliant ruler to a caricature of seduction and manipulation. The woman who had spoken nine languages, written treatises on medicine and law, and ruled the richest nation on earth had been transformed into nothing more than a beautiful temptress who had enchanted Julius Caesar and Mark Antony.

But Kathleen found Egyptian sources too, fragments of a different story. These described Cleopatra as "the greatest of her dynasty," a queen who had assumed the throne at eighteen and ruled with wisdom and strength for nearly two decades. The contradictions were staggering, and they fed Kathleen's growing obsession.

In Madrid, while her husband studied cardiology and their children played, Kathleen embarked on her archaeological education with the fervor of a convert. Every class opened new windows into the ancient world. She learned about excavation techniques, artifact analysis, and the painstaking work of reconstructing the past from fragments and clues. But it was the theoretical courses that truly excited her—the discussions about how archaeologists form hypotheses, test theories, and challenge established wisdom.

As she delved deeper into her studies, Kathleen began to develop her own theory about why Cleopatra's tomb had never been found. The answer, she believed, lay not in Alexandria where most scholars looked, but in understanding who Cleopatra really was. The queen hadn't just seen herself as a political ruler—she had believed she was the living embodiment of the goddess Isis, and that Mark Antony was the god Osiris.

This wasn't merely romantic symbolism. In ancient Egypt, divine identification carried profound implications for burial practices. If Cleopatra truly saw herself as Isis, then her final resting place would reflect that belief. She wouldn't be buried in a palace or royal necropolis like an ordinary pharaoh. She would choose a temple dedicated to her divine identity.

The theory was radical, and it flew in the face of conventional archaeological wisdom. But Kathleen had learned to trust her instincts, first in courtrooms and now in studying the past. She began sketching maps, identifying temples throughout Egypt that might fit her criteria. One site, in particular, caught her attention: Taposiris Magna, a semi-ruined temple about fifty kilometers west of Alexandria.

The more she researched, the more convinced she became. This wasn't just an intellectual exercise anymore—it was a calling. The woman who had reluctantly chosen law over archaeology was finally ready to follow her true passion. The only question was whether she had the courage to abandon everything she had built for a dream that might prove to be nothing more than wishful thinking.

By 2004, the decision was made. Kathleen Martinez would leave her successful law practice, her comfortable life, and her safe assumptions about the future. She would travel to Egypt and prove that the world's greatest archaeological mystery could be solved by a Dominican lawyer who had never stopped believing in the power of questions, evidence, and relentless determination.

The dreamer from Santo Domingo was about to become something far more dangerous: a woman with a theory, the skills to test it, and nothing left to lose.

Chapter 2: The Boy Who Dreamed Of Captain Nemo

The story begins on a sweltering June day in 1942, just six months after Pearl Harbor shattered America's peacetime illusions. In Wichita, Kansas, Robert Duane Ballard entered the world as the middle child of three, born into a family where dreams had to wrestle with harsh economic realities. His father, Chet Ballard, carried the weight of unfinished business—a brilliant mind who had been valedictorian of his high school class and started at the University of Washington, only to watch his college dreams crumble when the money ran out.

But Chet refused to let circumstance define his family's future. Working as a flight test engineer, he moved his young family from the flat wheat fields of Kansas to the Mojave Desert of California, where he tested cutting-edge aircraft alongside legendary pilot Chuck Yeager. For young Bob, this wasn't just a relocation—it was his first introduction to the intersection of human ambition and technological innovation that would define his entire life.

The desert years shaped something fundamental in Bob's character. His mother, Harriett, was the steady force who held the family together while Chet chased aviation's newest frontiers. She saw the restless energy in her son that others might have labeled problematic—what we now understand as dyslexia and hyperactivity—and channeled it into productive exploration. Bob learned early that if you wanted something beyond your basic needs, you had to earn it. By age ten, he was managing his own budget, working after-school jobs from paper routes to lawn mowing, understanding that dreams required sweat equity.

But it was the family's next move in 1948 that would alter the trajectory of Bob's life forever. San Diego beckoned with its promise of ocean breezes and endless Pacific horizons. They settled into a modest duplex within walking distance of a fishing pier and beach. "For me, that's where my life began," Ballard would later recall, and those words carry the weight of absolute truth.

While other kids his age were playing conventional games, Bob was discovering an underwater universe in the tidal pools along Mission Bay. Hour after hour, he'd crouch beside these miniature ecosystems, watching hermit crabs scramble across rocky surfaces and sea anemones wave in the gentle current. His neighbors worked at the Scripps Institution of Oceanography in nearby La Jolla, and their dinner-table conversations about deep-sea research filtered into Bob's consciousness like seeds taking root in fertile ground.

Then came the moment that would crystallize everything. At twelve years old, Bob walked into a movie theater to see Walt Disney's "20,000 Leagues Under the Sea." As Captain Nemo and his crew walked across the ocean floor in their diving suits, something clicked into place with an almost audible snap. "I watched the actors walking on the bottom of the ocean, and it was the first time I really thought about what is under the horizon," he remembers. "It excited me and when I learned there was a career in oceanography, I knew that's what I wanted to pursue."

The film wasn't just entertainment for Bob—it was revelation. Jules Verne's vision of underwater exploration, brought to vivid life by Disney's technical wizardry, offered a roadmap for a life he hadn't even known was possible. While his peers were drawn to cowboys or astronauts, Bob had found his calling in the mysterious depths that covered most of Earth's surface.

But dreams don't automatically translate into opportunities, especially for a hyperactive kid from a middle-class family in 1950s California. Bob channeled his oceanic obsession into practical steps, learning to scuba dive as a teenager and spending every possible moment in or near the water. His parents, recognizing the intensity of his passion, connected him with oceanographers at Scripps Institution. These weren't casual introductions—they were life-changing encounters that allowed Bob to participate in short research expeditions while still in high school.

By the time Bob enrolled at the University of California, Santa Barbara, he was no ordinary college freshman. He came with purpose, majoring in geology and chemistry with minors in mathematics and physics. But he wasn't just an academic—he played basketball and volleyball, served as junior class president, joined Sigma Alpha Epsilon fraternity, and completed the Army ROTC program. This wasn't the resume of someone simply going through the motions. This was a young man building the foundation for something extraordinary.

The year 1962 brought an opportunity that would prove pivotal. Bob began working part-time with Andreas Rechnitzer's Ocean Systems Group at North American Aviation, where his father served as chief engineer for the Minuteman missile program. It was here that Bob got his first taste of the engineering challenges involved in deep-sea exploration. The company was competing to build a revolutionary submersible called Alvin for the Woods Hole Oceanographic Institution. Though North American's proposal would ultimately fail, Bob's exposure to the project planted seeds that would bloom spectacularly in the years ahead.

Navy Service and Deep-Sea Calling (1965-1975)

Graduating in 1965 with undergraduate degrees in chemistry and geology, Bob found himself at a crossroads that millions of young American men faced during the Vietnam era. His ROTC commission meant military service was inevitable, but Bob saw opportunity where others might see obligation. When called to active duty in 1967, he made a request that would reshape not just his own future, but the entire field of underwater exploration: he asked to transfer from the Army to the Navy.

The Navy granted his request and assigned him as a liaison between the Office of Naval Research and the Woods Hole Oceanographic Institution in Massachusetts. This wasn't just a job assignment—it was like sending a kid to work in a candy factory. Woods Hole was the epicenter of American oceanographic research, and Bob found himself at the intersection of cutting-edge science and military necessity.

But first came graduate school and an unexpected detour that would prove surprisingly relevant to his future career. Bob earned his master's degree in geophysics from the University of Hawaii's Institute of Geophysics, where he spent his days doing something that might have seemed completely unrelated to deep-sea geology—training porpoises and whales. The experience was far from frivolous. Working with these intelligent marine mammals taught Bob about underwater behavior, navigation, and the complex challenges of operating in an alien environment. These lessons would prove invaluable when he later began working with underwater vehicles that needed to navigate the ocean's depths with similar precision and intelligence.

Returning to Andreas Rechnitzer's Ocean Systems Group at North American Aviation, Bob continued his education while immersing himself in the technical challenges of deep-sea exploration. He began working toward a Ph.D. in marine geology at the University of Southern California, but active duty called before he could complete it. This interruption, which might have derailed another person's career, instead positioned Bob perfectly for his life's work.

At Woods Hole, Bob encountered Alvin, the submersible his former employer had failed to build. Now owned by the Navy and operated by Woods Hole, Alvin represented everything Bob had dreamed about since watching Captain Nemo on the big screen fifteen years earlier. But this wasn't fantasy—this was a real vehicle capable of carrying humans to depths previously accessible only to imagination.

Bob's role initially involved convincing organizations and scientists to fund and use Alvin for undersea research. This meant he had to become more than just a scientist—he had to become a salesman, advocate, and visionary. The early 1970s were a skeptical time for manned submersibles. Many in the scientific community questioned whether these expensive, complex vehicles could justify their cost compared to traditional research methods.

Bob's first dive in a submersible came in 1969 aboard the Ben Franklin (PX-15) off the coast of Florida during a Woods Hole expedition. Descending through the water column in the protective embrace of a pressure vessel, watching the surface light fade to blue and then to black, Bob experienced something that would become as familiar as breathing—the transition from the known world of surface and sky to the alien landscape of the deep ocean.

In 1970, he began his own field mapping project of the Gulf of Maine for his doctoral dissertation, which he would eventually complete at the University of Rhode Island in 1974. This project combined traditional surface-based research with the revolutionary capabilities of Alvin. Using an air gun that sent sound waves underwater to determine the underlying structure of the ocean floor, paired with Alvin's ability to find and recover specific samples from the bedrock, Bob demonstrated the unique advantages that human-occupied submersibles could bring to marine geology.

But it was his involvement in Project FAMOUS (French-American Mid-Ocean Undersea Study) in 1974 that would establish Bob as a serious player in deep-sea exploration. This ambitious international collaboration brought together American and French submersibles to explore the Mid-Atlantic Ridge, the underwater mountain chain that marks where the Atlantic Ocean is slowly spreading apart.

Project FAMOUS was make-or-break time for manned submersibles. As the expedition was being planned, Maurice Ewing, one of the giants of oceanography, pointed his finger directly at Bob and delivered a warning that carried the weight of scientific history: "If you fail, we'll melt down Alvin's pressure sphere into titanium paper clips."

The pressure was immense, but so was the opportunity. Bob served as a geologist diver in Alvin, spending hours on the seafloor in a landscape that no human had ever seen. The volcanic terrain was both beautiful and alien, with fresh lava flows creating glass-like surfaces that reflected Alvin's lights. They mapped underwater canyons, collected rock samples, and proved beyond doubt that manned submersibles could effectively explore the most challenging terrain on Earth.

One terrifying moment during Project FAMOUS nearly ended Bob's career before it fully began. While investigating a seafloor fissure, Alvin became stuck, wedged between walls of volcanic rock with Bob and the crew trapped inside. As pilot Jack Donnelly worked frantically to free the submersible, Bob watched the pressure gauges and calculated their remaining life support. The experience would have been enough to send many people back to dry land permanently. For Bob, it was confirmation that he was exactly where he belonged.

Project FAMOUS succeeded spectacularly, proving that submersibles could map underwater terrain with the same precision that geologists achieved on land. The expedition brought together scientists and media representatives, introducing the general public to the idea that humans could explore the deepest parts of the ocean. Bob had helped win the argument for manned deep-sea exploration, but the greatest discoveries were still ahead.

The Hydrothermal Breakthrough (1975-1980)

By 1975, Bob had established himself as one of the leading advocates for manned submersible research, but the oceanographic community was still searching for the kind of breakthrough discovery that would justify the enormous costs and risks of deep-sea exploration. The theory of plate tectonics suggested that hydrothermal vents—underwater geysers of hot, mineral-rich water—should exist along mid-ocean ridges, but no one had actually seen them in action.

The search began with a joint French-American expedition called Phere, searching for hydrothermal vents over the Mid-Atlantic Ridge in 1975. Despite careful planning and the best available technology, the expedition found no active vents. It was a frustrating reminder that the ocean kept most of its secrets well hidden.

But failure often plants the seeds of future success. Based on earlier expeditions that had found temperature anomalies and unusual mineral deposits, scientists identified the Galápagos Rift as a promising location. In February 1977, Bob found himself aboard the research vessel Knorr, 400 miles off the South American coast, staring at photographs that would change everything.

The photos had been taken by ANGUS (Acoustic-Navigated Geological Underwater Survey), a deep-towed camera system that Bob's team had deployed 8,000 feet below the surface. As Bob studied the grainy black-and-white images, something caught his eye that made his pulse quicken. "I think there's shimmering water right over here to the left, coming out right off the top," he told his colleagues.

The images showed something else that was even more intriguing—dense clusters of white objects scattered across the seafloor. They looked like clams, but that seemed impossible. What could possibly support large populations of shellfish in the absolute darkness of the deep ocean, miles from any source of sunlight?

On February 17, 1977, Alvin dove to investigate, carrying pilot Jack Donnelly along with scientists Jack Corliss from Oregon State University and Tjeerd van Andel from Stanford. As they reached their target coordinates, the three men entered what Bob would later describe as "another world."

"Coming out of small cracks cutting across the lava terrain was warm, shimmering water that quickly turned a cloudy blue as manganese and other chemicals in solution began to precipitate out of the warm water," Bob wrote. Alvin's temperature sensors registered 8°C (46°F) at the bottom of the sea—significantly warmer than the near-freezing temperatures typical of deep ocean water.

They had found the first confirmed hydrothermal vent. But that was just the beginning of the surprises.

As Alvin maneuvered around the vent site, the crew encountered life forms that seemed to belong to an alien planet. Foot-long clams clustered around the warm-water vents. Giant tube worms, some reaching six feet in length, swayed in the current with their bright red plume-like heads resembling underwater tulips. Purple octopi moved through gardens of strange creatures that had never been seen before.

This wasn't just a geological discovery—it was a biological revolution. For the first time in Earth's history, scientists had discovered an ecosystem that existed completely independent of sunlight. These creatures survived through chemosynthesis, using bacteria to convert the hydrogen sulfide and other chemicals in the vent water into food energy.

Bob and his team had fundamentally changed our understanding of where life could exist. The discovery suggested that similar ecosystems might exist around hydrothermal vents throughout the world's oceans, and even raised possibilities about life existing in similar environments on other planets.

The scientific community was electrified, but Bob wasn't finished. In 1979, as part of the RISE (Rivera Submersible Experiments) project on the East Pacific Rise west of Mexico, he made another discovery that was even more dramatic. When Alvin investigated a site identified by deep-towed cameras, the crew observed black "smoke" billowing from towering mineral chimneys on the seafloor.

These "black smokers" were shooting superheated water at temperatures reaching 350°C (662°F)—hot enough to melt lead. The temperature reading nearly destroyed Alvin's instruments, and the sight was so otherworldly that it seemed like peering into the Earth's furnace through cracks in the seafloor.

Bob would later say, "Finding hydrothermal vents beats the hell out of finding the Titanic." His mother agreed, commenting years later, "It's too bad you found that rusty old boat... they're only going to remember you for finding [it]."

But Bob's mother was wrong about one thing. The scientific community understood the significance of what he had accomplished. The discovery of hydrothermal vents opened entirely new fields of research in biology, chemistry, geology, and geophysics. It suggested new theories about how life might have originated on Earth and where it might exist elsewhere in the universe.

By 1980, Bob Ballard had established himself as one of the world's leading deep-sea explorers. He had proven the value of manned submersibles, discovered new forms of life, and opened windows into processes that had been hidden in the deep ocean for millions of years. The boy who had dreamed of walking on the ocean floor like Captain Nemo had done something even more remarkable—he had revealed that the real ocean was far more wondrous than anything Jules Verne had imagined.

The stage was set for the next phase of his career, when he would combine his expertise in deep-sea exploration with his growing interest in maritime archaeology. The "rusty old boat" his mother mentioned—the RMS Titanic—was waiting in the North Atlantic depths, ready to make Bob Ballard a household name around the world. But that achievement would never diminish the scientific significance of his earlier work. He had already discovered worlds beneath the waves that no one had known existed, proving that the ocean's deepest secrets were worth pursuing no matter how difficult the journey might be.

Chapter 3: Martinez's First Steps into the Sands of Egypt

The Dominican Republic passport felt impossibly light in Kathleen Martinez's trembling hands as she stood in the immigration line at Cairo International Airport in 2002. Around her, seasoned travelers shuffled through the early morning routine with practiced ease, but Martinez felt like she was stepping through a portal into another world. Her cousin stood beside her, equally nervous, both women acutely aware that they were about to attempt something that bordered on the impossible.

The immigration officer's eyes narrowed as he examined Martinez's burgundy passport. In his weathered hands, the document looked foreign, almost suspicious. He turned it over, studying the embossed seal, then looked up at Martinez with undisguised skepticism.

"Mickey Mouse," he said dismissively, his English heavily accented but cutting. The words hung in the air like a slap. Martinez felt her heart sink as she realized what was happening—to this man, her Dominican Republic passport might as well have been fake. The Dominican Republic didn't have an embassy in Egypt, and to him, that meant her country barely existed on the diplomatic map. What followed was a nightmare that would have sent most people straight back home on the next flight. Martinez was detained, separated from her cousin, and led to a stark questioning room where fluorescent lights buzzed overhead like angry insects. Hours crawled by. She thought about her family back in Santo Domingo, who had begged her not to make this trip. Her mother's tears. Her father's warnings about the dangers of traveling alone to a country that didn't recognize their existence.

But something steel-hard inside Martinez refused to break. She had spent years preparing for this moment, researching in her father's library, mapping out her theory about Cleopatra's burial site. She wasn't going to let airport bureaucracy destroy her dream before it had even begun.

When officials finally emerged and ordered her and her cousin into a van that would supposedly take them to their hotel, Martinez's lawyer instincts kicked in. Something felt wrong. Very wrong. She stalled for time, asking to use the restroom, waiting until the airport shops opened. Her heart hammered against her ribs as she made what felt like the most important decision of her life. Instead of getting into that van, Martinez ducked into the first open shop she saw—a travel agency. The startled agent behind the counter looked up as this Dominican woman in rumpled clothes fell into his chair and desperately requested a car, a driver, and most importantly, a Spanish-speaking guide.

It was a moment of pure instinct that would change everything. The guide she hired knew someone who knew someone who worked as a scheduling secretary for Zahi Hawass, then Egypt's most powerful archaeologist and director of the Supreme Council of Antiquities. Within two minutes of explaining her theory, Martinez had secured something that typically took months to arrange—a two-month permit to visit temples usually reserved for archaeological research.

"In archaeology, two months is nothing," Martinez would later reflect. But for a woman who had just talked her way out of detention and convinced one of the world's most renowned archaeologists to take a chance on her wild theory, two months felt like a lifetime of possibility.

During those precious weeks, Martinez visited temple after temple, her notebooks filling with observations, measurements, and growing conviction. She had identified 21 potential burial sites for Cleopatra based on ancient Roman texts, particularly the writings of Strabo. Each location had to meet specific criteria—it needed to be associated with the goddess Isis, accessible from Alexandria within a day's travel, and positioned in a place where Cleopatra could have hidden her body from the Romans who so desperately wanted to parade her through the streets of Rome. When Martinez finally arrived at Taposiris Magna, roughly 30 miles west of Alexandria, she felt something she had never experienced before. The semi-destroyed temple sat on the edge of what had once been Lake Mariout, its limestone blocks scattered across the sandy ground like pieces of a giant puzzle. Most archaeologists had dismissed this site as uninteresting, an incomplete temple that held little promise for significant discoveries.

But Martinez saw something different. She sat against the remains of an ancient column, surrounded by rubble and the whispers of desert wind, and wept. Not from despair, but from overwhelming certainty. "This is it," she whispered to herself. "This is where she is."

The theory that would revolutionize Cleopatra scholarship was elegant in its logic. Cleopatra had fashioned herself as the living embodiment of Isis, the goddess of magic, motherhood, and rebirth. If she were planning her final resting place, knowing that the Romans wanted her body as a trophy, she would choose somewhere sacred to Isis, somewhere close enough to Alexandria to be reachable, but far enough from the royal quarters to avoid Roman detection. Taposiris Magna—the "Great Tomb of Osiris"—was perfect. As the burial place of Osiris, husband of Isis, it held profound religious significance. The temple complex had been built by Ptolemy II, Cleopatra's ancestor, making it a family site. Most importantly, it was a place the Romans would never think to look.

But standing in that ruined temple, Martinez faced the crushing reality of her situation. She was a criminal lawyer from a small Caribbean island with no archaeological credentials, no university backing, and no funding. Who would listen to her? Who would give her permission to excavate? The magnitude of what she was attempting hit her like a physical blow.

Then something inside her shifted. The same stubborn determination that had carried her through law school at 18, that had built her successful practice, that had brought her to Egypt despite everyone's warnings—that fire flared to life. She stopped crying and made a vow that would define the next two decades of her life: "I have to fight until they tell me yes, if it takes the rest of my life."

Taposiris Magna: The Temple That Changed Everything (2004-2005)

Back in Santo Domingo, Martinez faced skepticism that bordered on ridicule. Her colleagues in the legal profession thought she had lost her mind. Egyptian archaeology? A Dominican woman with no training trying to solve one of history's greatest mysteries? The whispers followed her through the halls of the courthouse, but Martinez had learned to tune out doubt. She threw herself into preparation with the same methodical approach she used for her most complex criminal cases. With support from the Universidad Católica Santo Domingo, she crafted a formal proposal that would make history—the first time Egypt had ever granted an excavation license to a Latin American country.

The significance of this couldn't be overstated. Egypt guarded its archaeological treasures jealously, typically only allowing established European or American institutions to conduct major excavations. For a small Caribbean nation to receive such permission was unprecedented. It was a testament to both Martinez's persuasive abilities and the compelling nature of her theory. What she discovered about Taposiris Magna during her research only strengthened her conviction. The temple was an anomaly in every possible way. For centuries, archaeologists had searched for its foundation deposits—the ceremonial caches buried during construction to bless the building and commemorate its builder. These deposits were crucial for dating structures and understanding their purpose. At Taposiris Magna, no one had found them.

In archaeological terms, a foundation plate or deposit is like a birth certificate for an ancient building. It contains precious objects, inscriptions, and often miniature tools that reveal when the structure was built, by whom, and for what purpose. The fact that no one had found these deposits at Taposiris Magna in over a century of intermittent exploration was deeply puzzling. Martinez approached the mystery like a detective. If the foundation deposits were there, they would be buried at specific locations according to ancient Egyptian ritual practices. She studied the architectural patterns of other Ptolemaic temples, analyzed the topography of the site, and made educated guesses about where the builders would have placed these crucial caches.

When she finally returned to Egypt in 2004 with proper funding and permits, Martinez was a different person than the desperate woman who had been detained at Cairo Airport two years earlier. Now she carried diplomatic credentials as the Dominican Republic's first Minister of Culture to Egypt, a position created specifically to support her groundbreaking work. The burgundy passport that had once been dismissed as "Mickey Mouse" now commanded respect.

Her first major breakthrough came within three months of beginning excavations—a speed that stunned the archaeological community. Where others had searched for centuries without success, Martinez and her team found the foundation deposits of Taposiris Magna embedded in clay tablets made of lapis lazuli, turquoise, and glass. The writing on these fragile artifacts was barely legible, worn by centuries of desert sand and shifting earth. But Martinez could make out the crucial words written in ancient Greek: "Basileosus, Ptolomios"—King Ptolemy. Carbon dating revealed the deposits were laid around 280-270 BCE by Ptolemy IV, making this a direct link between the temple site and Cleopatra's family line. For the first time in over 2,000 years, the world knew definitively who had built Taposiris Magna and when.

But the real revelation came from what the inscriptions revealed about the temple's purpose. The hieroglyphics and Greek text indicated that this wasn't just any temple—it was specifically dedicated to Isis, the goddess with whom Cleopatra had so powerfully identified. The pieces of Martinez's theory were falling into place with almost supernatural precision.

The discovery electrified the archaeological world and vindicated Martinez's years of preparation. Here was a woman with no formal training in Egyptology who had solved a mystery that had stumped experts for generations. The foundation deposits didn't just prove the temple's age and builder—they provided the first concrete evidence that Taposiris Magna was exactly what Martinez had theorized: a sacred site dedicated to Isis, built by Cleopatra's ancestors, perfectly positioned to serve as a hidden burial ground for Egypt's last queen.

Early Discoveries and Setbacks (2005-2010)

The Egyptian government's ultimatum came like a thunderbolt in 2005: Martinez had exactly two months to produce significant findings, or her excavation permit would be revoked forever. Two months to justify years of preparation, international agreements, and her entire theory. Two months to prove that a Dominican lawyer's obsession with ancient Egypt wasn't just the fantasy of an amateur archaeologist. The pressure was crushing. Martinez had sold her law practice, moved to Egypt, and staked her entire professional reputation at this moment. If she failed, she wouldn't just lose face—she would lose everything. The international media was watching, skeptics were waiting for her failure, and the clock was ticking with merciless precision.

Working fourteen-hour days under the scorching Egyptian sun, Martinez and her team excavated with desperate intensity. The sand seemed to mock their efforts, revealing pottery shards and animal bones but nothing that would convince the authorities of the site's significance. With each passing day, the deadline loomed larger, the weight of potential failure growing heavier. Then, with exactly one hour remaining before the government shutdown of her project,

Martinez's team made a discovery that would change everything. Deep beneath the temple floor, they found the entrance to an underground tunnel system. Not just any tunnel—a carefully constructed passageway that extended from the temple complex toward the Mediterranean Sea.

The timing was so dramatic, so impossibly close to the deadline, that it seemed almost scripted. But there it was: concrete proof that Taposiris Magna held secrets worth exploring. The Egyptian authorities, impressed by this last-minute revelation, granted Martinez an extension that would eventually stretch into decades. That tunnel discovery marked the beginning of what would become one of the most extraordinary archaeological projects of the 21st century. As Martinez's team began exploring the underground network, they realized they had found something unprecedented. The tunnel was over 4,200 feet long, meticulously carved through solid rock, leading directly from the temple toward the sea. No similar construction had ever been found at an Egyptian temple site.

The implications were staggering. Why would ancient builders create such an elaborate underground system? What were they hiding? Martinez's theory provided a compelling answer: this tunnel had been designed to transport Cleopatra's body from the temple to a hidden burial location, possibly even beneath the Mediterranean itself.

In 2006, just a year after nearly losing everything, Martinez made her next breakthrough discovery. Deep within the tunnel system, her team found the first coins bearing Cleopatra's image ever discovered at an archaeological site. These weren't random artifacts—they were carefully placed offerings, hidden in sealed chambers that had remained undisturbed for over two millennia. The coins were a revelation on multiple levels. First, they provided direct evidence that Cleopatra had been associated with this site during her lifetime. Second, their placement suggested ritual significance, as if they had been left as offerings or markers. Most importantly, they validated Martinez's methodology—her careful analysis of ancient texts and her intuitive understanding of Cleopatra's mindset had led her to exactly the right place.

But success came with its own challenges. Martinez was funding these excavations largely from her own resources, drawing on the profits from her former law practice and later securing Dominican government support. The scale of the project was expanding beyond anything she had originally imagined. What had begun as a targeted search for a tomb was revealing an entire underground complex that would require decades to fully explore. The financial pressure was relentless. Archaeological excavations are expensive under the best circumstances, requiring specialized equipment, expert personnel, security, and preservation materials. Martinez was attempting to fund a major international dig while maintaining the highest scientific standards—all while operating from a small Caribbean nation with limited archaeological resources.

Yet she refused offers of funding from major American and European universities, a decision that puzzled many in the archaeological community. Martinez was determined that this remain a Dominican-Egyptian project, with all discoveries credited to her homeland. She understood that this might be the only chance for a Latin American nation to make a mark in Egyptology, and she wasn't going to let that opportunity slip away.

By 2010, Martinez had established a permanent presence at Taposiris Magna. Her team had discovered not just coins, but alabaster busts, pottery fragments, and architectural elements that painted a picture of a site far more significant than anyone had imagined. Each artifact told a story, each discovery raised new questions, and each season brought Martinez closer to answering the ultimate question: was Cleopatra really buried here?

The early discoveries had transformed Martinez from an unknown amateur into a recognized figure in international archaeology. Her work was being featured in National Geographic, her theories were being debated in academic journals, and her story was inspiring a new generation of archaeologists from underrepresented backgrounds. But perhaps most importantly, those first five years had proven something that Martinez had always believed: that passion, preparation, and persistence could overcome institutional barriers and conventional wisdom. She had taken a theory that existed only in her mind, tested it against the harsh reality of the Egyptian desert, and emerged with evidence that the archaeological establishment could no longer ignore.

The quest that had begun with a detention room in Cairo Airport had evolved into something far greater than the search for a single tomb. Martinez was rewriting the rules of who could be an archaeologist, challenging assumptions about where important discoveries might be found, and proving that the most revolutionary insights sometimes come from the most unexpected sources.

Standing in her excavation site as 2010 drew to a close, Martinez could look back on a half-decade that had transformed both her life and her chosen field. The girl who had grown up in her father's library, dreaming of ancient Egypt, had become the woman whose discoveries were reshaping how the world understood one of history's most famous figures. But she also knew that her greatest challenges still lay ahead. The tunnel beckoned, mysterious and full of promise, leading toward secrets that had waited over two thousand years to be revealed.

Chapter 4: The Titanic Hunter's Secret Mission

The salt air whipped across Robert Ballard's face as he watched $600,000 worth of equipment disappear into the black depths of the Atlantic. It was October 1977, and his first serious attempt to find the Titanic had just become an expensive lesson in the brutal realities of deep-sea exploration. The 3,000-foot drilling pipe attached to the Alcoa Seaprobe had snapped like a twig, taking with it not just sophisticated cameras and sonar equipment, but also Ballard's confidence that finding the world's most famous shipwreck would be easy.

Standing on deck as the broken pipe plummeted toward the seafloor, Ballard felt the weight of failure crushing down on him. This wasn't just about losing equipment—it was about watching his dream sink into the same abyss that had swallowed the Titanic sixty-five years earlier. The scientific community at Woods Hole had already been skeptical of his ambitions, viewing him as something of a showman seeking publicity rather than serious science. Now they had concrete evidence to support their doubts.

The Failed First Attempt (1977)

The Seaprobe expedition had started with such promise. Ballard had convinced the Alcoa Aluminum Company to let him use their deep-sea salvage vessel, essentially a floating drilling rig equipped with a massive derrick capable of lowering equipment to the ocean floor. The concept was revolutionary for its time—instead of sending down expensive manned submersibles, they would lower a pod containing cameras and sonar equipment attached to the end of the drilling pipe, extending it 60 feet at a time until it reached the Titanic's resting place over two miles below.

The technology seemed foolproof on paper. The equipment pod could be maneuvered like a deep-sea puppet, controlled from the surface while sending back live images of the seafloor. If they found something promising, a mechanical claw could be attached to retrieve samples. Ballard had estimated the entire discovery would take just 10 to 12 days—a calculation that would prove laughably optimistic.

But the ocean has a way of humbling even the most confident explorers. On what should have been a routine deployment, a mistake in the rigging caused catastrophic failure. The pipe snapped with a sharp crack that echoed across the water, and Ballard watched helplessly as his equipment vanished into the depths. At that moment, he realized that finding the Titanic would require far more than conventional thinking and existing technology.

The failure stung deeply, not just because of the financial loss, but because it forced Ballard to confront the limitations of traditional deep-sea exploration methods. The experience taught him that the ocean floor was not a place for clunky, inflexible equipment. What he needed was something more agile, more responsive—something that could dance through the underwater terrain rather than lumber across it like a mechanical giant.

As news of the failed expedition spread through the oceanographic community, Ballard found himself increasingly isolated. Funding sources dried up, colleagues distanced themselves, and the dream of finding the Titanic seemed to be slipping away like the broken pipe that had started this nightmare. But failure has a way of crystallizing vision, and Ballard began to imagine a different approach entirely.

The Seaprobe disaster became the catalyst for one of the most important innovations in underwater exploration history. Ballard returned to Woods Hole with a radical new concept brewing in his mind—why risk human lives or expensive drilling equipment when you could send down unmanned vehicles that could stream live video back to the surface?

Working with engineers and fellow researchers, Ballard began developing what would eventually become the Argo/Jason system. The idea was elegantly simple: a remotely operated vehicle equipped with powerful cameras and lights, tethered to the surface ship by fiber-optic cable that could transmit high-definition images in real-time. Unlike the cumbersome drilling approach, these robots could glide over the seafloor like underwater aircraft, covering vast areas while their operators remained safely on the surface.

The concept represented a fundamental shift in deep-sea exploration philosophy. Instead of sending humans down in pressure-resistant submersibles—a journey that took hours just to reach the bottom—scientists could now explore the abyss from the comfort and safety of a ship's control room. Multiple experts could analyze discoveries simultaneously, and the fiber-optic connection meant that findings could be shared with researchers around the world in real-time.

Ballard's vision went beyond just finding shipwrecks. He saw telepresence technology as a way to democratize ocean exploration, allowing students in classrooms to accompany scientists on deep-sea expeditions. The failed Seaprobe mission had taught him that the future of underwater exploration lay not in bigger, more powerful equipment, but in smarter, more flexible technology that worked with the ocean rather than against it.

By the early 1980s, Ballard's team had transformed his post-failure vision into reality. Argo emerged as a sleek, unmanned vehicle about the size of a small car, bristling with cameras, sonar equipment, and powerful lights capable of illuminating the pitch-black depths of the ocean. The system represented a quantum leap in underwater exploration capability.

The heart of Argo's innovation lay in its fiber-optic cable connection to the surface. Unlike the copper cables used in earlier underwater vehicles, fiber-optics could transmit crystal-clear, high-definition video without the signal degradation that plagued older systems. For the first time in deep-sea exploration history, scientists on the surface could see the ocean floor with the same clarity as if they were looking through the window of a submersible.

But Argo was just one part of Ballard's revolutionary system. Tethered to the main vehicle was Jason, a smaller, more maneuverable robot that could detach and explore tight spaces, take close-up photographs, and collect samples while Argo provided the stable platform and communication link. The two-vehicle approach gave explorers unprecedented flexibility in examining underwater sites.

The development process had been grueling, requiring innovations in materials science, robotics, and underwater communications. Every component had to withstand crushing pressure, corrosive seawater, and the constant stress of deep-sea operations. Ballard and his team spent years perfecting the system, driven by the memory of that failed drilling pipe and the determination to prove that their new approach could succeed where traditional methods had failed.

While Ballard was perfecting his underwater robotics, the U.S. Navy was grappling with two of its most troubling Cold War mysteries. In the 1960s, two nuclear-powered submarines had been lost in the Atlantic Ocean under circumstances that remained unclear decades later. The USS Thresher had disappeared in 1963 with 129 men aboard, followed by the USS Scorpion in 1968, taking 99 sailors to their deaths.

These weren't just tragic accidents—they were potential national security disasters. Both submarines carried nuclear reactors, and the Navy had no idea whether these reactors posed an environmental threat or if sensitive technology could be compromised by Soviet forces. During the height of the Cold War, the possibility that the Scorpion had been sunk by enemy action couldn't be dismissed, and naval intelligence desperately needed to know what had really happened to their lost vessels.

The problem was that both submarines lay at depths between 10,000 and 15,000 feet—far beyond the reach of conventional diving or salvage operations. The Navy needed advanced deep-sea imaging technology to examine the wrecks and determine their condition, but existing equipment was inadequate for the task. Traditional underwater vehicles couldn't provide the detailed visual information required, and the risks of sending manned submersibles to such depths were enormous.

When Ballard approached the Navy in 1982 with his Argo system, it seemed like the answer to their prayers. Here was technology specifically designed for deep-sea reconnaissance, capable of providing real-time, high-definition images from depths that had previously been inaccessible. The Navy quickly recognized that Ballard's system represented their best chance of finally learning the fate of their lost submarines and assessing any potential security risks.

Operation Titanic: The Cover Story (1982-1985)

The meeting that would change maritime archaeology forever took place in a nondescript Pentagon office in 1982. Ballard sat across from Deputy Chief of Naval Operations Ronald Thunman, pitching his Argo system with the enthusiasm of a man who had spent years perfecting his vision. But Thunman wasn't particularly interested in finding the Titanic—he was focused on two nuclear submarines that had become Cold War ghosts.

"We'll fund your technology development," Thunman told Ballard, "but you're going to investigate the Thresher and Scorpion first." The admiral made it clear that the Navy's priority was determining the condition of the submarines' nuclear reactors and understanding how the vessels had been destroyed. Only after completing this classified mission would Ballard be free to pursue his Titanic obsession.

What followed was one of the most elaborate cover stories in Cold War history. Ballard would be temporarily recalled to active duty and placed in charge of a highly classified mission to examine the submarine wrecks. But to the outside world, he would be leading a joint French-American expedition to find the Titanic. The legendary passenger liner would serve as the perfect cover story, generating enough media interest to mask the true nature of the operation while providing plausible explanation for increased U.S. naval activity in the North Atlantic.

The USS Thresher represented one of the Navy's most advanced attack submarines when it disappeared during deep-diving tests on April 10, 1963. The vessel had been conducting routine trials 220 miles east of Cape Cod when communication was lost. The last transmission from the submarine was garbled and ominous: "Experiencing minor difficulty... have a positive up angle... attempting to blow." Then silence.

The Navy's subsequent search and rescue operation became a recovery mission when debris from the submarine was found on the ocean floor. The official investigation concluded that a piping failure had led to flooding, which caused the nuclear reactor to shut down automatically. Without power, the submarine couldn't surface and was crushed by water pressure as it sank beyond its maximum operating depth.

The USS Scorpion's fate was even more mysterious. The submarine had been returning from a routine patrol in the Mediterranean when it vanished 400 miles southwest of the Azores in May 1968. Unlike the Thresher, there had been no distress call, no indication of problems. The submarine simply disappeared with all 99 crew members, becoming one of four submarines lost worldwide that year in what became known as the "Year of the Submarine."

Theories about the Scorpion's destruction ranged from mechanical failure to Soviet attack. Some intelligence analysts believed the submarine had been torpedoed in retaliation for U.S. surveillance activities, while others suggested an onboard explosion or catastrophic hull failure. The truth lay buried two and a half miles beneath the Atlantic, waiting for technology advanced enough to reveal it.

For Ballard, examining these wrecks represented both a solemn duty and an incredible opportunity. The classified mission would provide funding for his Argo system while allowing him to test the technology under real operational conditions. But it also meant working under intense secrecy, knowing that any revelations about the submarines' condition could have significant implications for national security.

The stakes of Ballard's classified mission extended far beyond satisfying historical curiosity. Both lost submarines were powered by nuclear reactors, and after decades on the ocean floor, the Navy needed to know whether these reactors posed environmental or security risks. The reactor cores contained weapons-grade uranium, and there were legitimate concerns about potential radioactive contamination of the surrounding ocean.

More troubling from a strategic perspective was the possibility that Soviet forces had accessed the wreck sites. The submarines contained classified technology including sonar systems, nuclear propulsion details, and cryptographic equipment that could compromise U.S. naval operations if it fell into enemy hands. Intelligence analysts worried that the Soviets might be secretly studying the wreck sites, learning American submarine design secrets, or even recovering sensitive materials.

Ballard's mission was to conduct a comprehensive photographic survey of both wrecks, documenting their condition and searching for evidence of external damage that might indicate enemy action. The Argo system's advanced cameras could reveal details impossible to detect with earlier underwater vehicles, potentially answering questions that had haunted naval intelligence for decades.

The operation required extraordinary secrecy. Even members of Ballard's own team were not fully briefed on the mission's true purpose until they were already at sea. Cover stories had to be maintained at every level, from the ship's manifest to the research permits filed with international maritime authorities. The slightest leak could compromise not just the immediate mission, but ongoing Cold War submarine operations worldwide.

As Ballard prepared for the expedition, he knew he was carrying the weight of national security on his shoulders. The images his system captured could reshape understanding of submarine warfare, influence nuclear safety policies, and potentially reveal whether American sailors had died in enemy attacks. The pressure was immense, but so was the opportunity to prove that his revolutionary technology could succeed where conventional approaches had failed.

After completing the submarine surveys in the summer of 1985, Ballard faced a challenge that would test every lesson learned from his years of preparation. The Navy had allocated time for the Titanic search as part of maintaining his cover story, but the window was brutally small—just twelve days to find a shipwreck that had eluded searchers for over seven decades.

The timeframe seemed almost impossible. Previous expeditions by Texas millionaire Jack Grimm had spent more than forty days searching without success, using some of the most advanced sonar equipment available. Ballard would have less than two weeks to cover the vast search area and locate a target that countless others had missed.

But the submarine missions had taught Ballard something crucial about how shipwrecks behave as they sink. Both the Thresher and Scorpion had left extensive debris fields as they plummeted toward the ocean floor, with lighter materials scattered over areas much larger than the main hull sections. The debris trails created a much bigger target than the ships themselves—and the Titanic, which had broken apart during its sinking, should have left an even more extensive debris field.

This insight revolutionized Ballard's search strategy. Instead of looking for the intact ship sections, which would be like finding a needle in a haystack, he would search for the much larger debris field. Once found, the debris trail would lead directly to the main wreck site, just as it had with the submarines. It was a brilliant application of lessons learned during the classified missions, demonstrating how military research could benefit civilian exploration.

The psychological pressure of the twelve-day deadline was intense. Ballard's team worked in shifts, monitoring video feeds from Argo as it swept back and forth across the ocean floor two miles below. Everyone understood that this might be their only chance—if they failed to find the Titanic during this expedition, funding for future attempts would be virtually impossible to obtain.

At 12:48 AM on September 1, 1985, everything changed. Dr. Robert Ballard was reading in his cabin aboard the research vessel Knorr when the ship's cook burst through his door, barely able to contain his excitement. The overnight watch team had spotted something on the video feed from Argo—something that looked like it might be a ship's boiler.

Ballard threw on his flight suit over his pajamas and rushed to the control room, his heart pounding with anticipation and dread. After eight years of planning, technology development, and preparation, after the humiliation of the Seaprobe failure and the pressure of the classified submarine missions, everything came down to this moment. The grainy black-and-white image on the monitor showed a cylindrical object sitting on the otherwise smooth ocean floor.

"We realized it was definitely from the Titanic," Ballard later recalled, "and all bedlam broke loose." The control room erupted in celebration as team members recognized the distinctive boiler design that matched the ship's specifications. After 73 years of mystery, the world's most famous shipwreck had finally been found.

But even in that moment of triumph, Ballard was acutely aware of the secret that lay beneath his success. The technology that had made this discovery possible had been developed and funded for military purposes. The expedition that found the Titanic had been, first and foremost, a classified intelligence operation designed to investigate lost nuclear submarines during the Cold War.

As news of the discovery spread around the world, generating headlines and making Ballard an international celebrity, he was bound by military secrecy to maintain the fiction that finding the Titanic had always been his primary objective. The truth about Operation Titanic would remain classified for decades, known only to a handful of Navy officials and intelligence analysts who understood the real stakes of the mission.

Beyond the Titanic: A Legend Emerges (1985-2000)

The discovery of the Titanic transformed Robert Ballard from a respected oceanographer into a global celebrity, but fame came with its own burdens. Suddenly thrust into the media spotlight, he found himself fielding interview requests from around the world while carefully maintaining the cover story that had concealed his classified mission. Every question about the discovery required careful consideration—what could he reveal without compromising national security?

The public's fascination with the Titanic was immediate and overwhelming. The haunting images transmitted by Argo showed a ship frozen in time, its grand staircase collapsed but its basic structure remarkably preserved by the cold, oxygen-poor environment of the deep Atlantic. For the first time, people could see the reality of the disaster that had captivated imaginations for over seven decades.

But Ballard's success with the Titanic was just the beginning. The same technology and techniques that had located the famous liner could be applied to other maritime mysteries, and the oceanographer found himself in demand for increasingly ambitious underwater expeditions. Each new project built upon lessons learned from previous missions, pushing the boundaries of what was possible in deep-sea exploration.

In 1989, Ballard set his sights on another legendary shipwreck: the German battleship Bismarck, which had been sunk by British forces in 1941 after a dramatic chase across the North Atlantic. The massive warship lay at depths of over 15,000 feet—4,000 feet deeper than the Titanic—presenting new challenges for his underwater technology.

The Bismarck expedition was personal for Ballard in ways that went beyond professional achievement. His 21-year-old son Todd had joined the team as a crew member, eager to follow in his father's footsteps as an ocean explorer. The young man had inherited his father's fascination with the sea and showed promise as a researcher and expedition member.

The discovery of the Bismarck revealed a ship that, unlike the Titanic, appeared to have sunk largely intact. The battleship's massive hull showed evidence of battle damage from British shells and torpedoes, but Ballard's investigation suggested that the ship had ultimately been scuttled by its own crew rather than sunk purely by enemy action. The finding provided new insights into one of World War II's most famous naval battles.

But triumph turned to tragedy just three weeks after the expedition ended. Todd Ballard was killed in a car accident, devastating his father and casting a shadow over what should have been another career-defining success. The loss of his son profoundly affected Ballard's perspective on exploration and life, adding a personal dimension of grief to his professional achievements.

The tragedy reinforced Ballard's commitment to using technology to keep explorers safe while pushing the boundaries of discovery. Todd's death served as a painful reminder that exploration always carries risks, and that the underwater robotics technology his father had pioneered represented more than just scientific advancement—it was a way to satisfy human curiosity while protecting human lives.

The thousands of letters Ballard received from students after discovering the Titanic inspired him to create one of the most innovative educational programs in science history. The JASON Project, launched in 1989, used the same telepresence technology that had found the famous shipwreck to bring live ocean exploration into classrooms around the world.

The concept was revolutionary: instead of simply reading about underwater discoveries in textbooks, students could participate in real expeditions through live video and audio feeds transmitted via satellite and later the internet. Children sitting in classrooms could watch as Ballard's robots explored ancient shipwrecks, hydrothermal vents, and underwater volcanoes, asking questions and making observations alongside professional scientists.

The JASON Project democratized ocean exploration in ways that would have been impossible just a few years earlier. Students from inner-city schools could dive to the deepest parts of the ocean, while rural classrooms could explore underwater archaeological sites on the other side of the world. The program reached millions of students over its decades of operation, inspiring countless young people to pursue careers in science and exploration.

For Ballard, the project represented a way to honor his son's memory while ensuring that future generations would continue pushing the boundaries of human knowledge. The same fiber-optic technology that had been developed for military reconnaissance missions was now being used to educate children and foster scientific curiosity worldwide.

Ballard's success with the Titanic and Bismarck opened doors to increasingly prestigious projects, each building upon the technological and operational expertise gained from previous missions. In 1998, he discovered the aircraft carrier USS Yorktown, which had been sunk during the Battle of Midway in 1942. The discovery provided new insights into one of the Pacific War's most crucial engagements.

Perhaps even more historically significant was Ballard's 2002 discovery of PT-109, the Navy patrol boat commanded by future President John F. Kennedy during World War II.

Kennedy's heroic actions after the boat was sunk by a Japanese destroyer had become legendary, but the exact location of the wreck had remained unknown for decades.

The PT-109 discovery involved more than just finding another shipwreck—it connected Ballard with history in the most personal way possible. He met with Biuku Gasa and Eroni Kumana, the Solomon Islander scouts who had rescued Kennedy and his surviving crew members after the sinking. The encounter bridged decades and cultures, demonstrating how maritime archaeology could bring together people separated by time and geography.

Each discovery added to Ballard's reputation while refining his technological capabilities. The underwater robotics systems continued to evolve, becoming more sophisticated and reliable with each expedition. What had started as a response to the failed Seaprobe mission had become the foundation for an entire new field of exploration.

By the 1990s, Ballard had become one of the most recognizable scientists in the world, but he was increasingly eager to establish his own research institution where he could pursue projects without the constraints of larger organizational structures. In 1997, he left Woods Hole Oceanographic Institution to found the Institute for Exploration in Mystic, Connecticut.

The new institute represented Ballard's vision of how modern exploration should be conducted. Combining cutting-edge technology with innovative educational programs, the facility became a center for both research and public engagement. The same telepresence technology that had found the Titanic was used to create interactive exhibits where visitors could participate in live underwater expeditions.

In 2002, Ballard accepted a position as professor of oceanography at the University of Rhode Island, where he established the Institute for Archaeological Oceanography. The new position allowed him to train the next generation of underwater explorers while continuing his own research projects. His students learned not just the technical aspects of deep-sea exploration, but also the importance of sharing discoveries with the broader public.

Throughout this period, Ballard maintained his connections to the military and intelligence communities that had made his early successes possible. The classified submarine missions of the 1980s remained secret, but the relationships and expertise developed during those operations continued to inform his work. The line between civilian exploration and national security research remained blurred, reflecting the complex realities of Cold War-era science.

The transformation from the young oceanographer who had watched his equipment disappear into the Atlantic in 1977 to the globally recognized explorer of the 2000s represented more than just personal success. Ballard had revolutionized underwater exploration, inspired millions of students, and demonstrated how military research could benefit civilian science. His story embodied the potential for technology to expand human knowledge while serving multiple purposes simultaneously.

As the 20th century drew to a close, Ballard looked back on a career that had fundamentally changed how humans explore the ocean depths. The same innovative spirit that had emerged from the failure of the Seaprobe expedition continued to drive new discoveries and technological advances. But perhaps most importantly, his work has shown that the greatest discoveries often emerge from the intersection of scientific curiosity, technological innovation, and national service—even when that service must remain hidden from public view for decades.

The boy who had dreamed of becoming Captain Nemo had surpassed even his childhood hero's achievements, using advanced technology to explore realms that had been previously inaccessible to human knowledge. And somewhere in the depths of the Atlantic, the Titanic continued its eternal rest, no longer lost but now serving as a bridge between the past and future of human exploration.

Chapter 5: Twenty Years In The Desert

The Egyptian desert is unforgiving. It strips away illusions, tests every theory, and humbles the proud. For Kathleen Martinez, it became both sanctuary and battlefield—a place where a Dominican lawyer's radical theories would either crumble into sand or reshape our understanding of history's most enigmatic queen.

Building the Dominican-Egyptian Mission (2005-2015)

When Martinez first approached the Egyptian authorities in 2005, she carried more than just archaeological theories. She carried the weight of an entire nation's aspirations on her shoulders. Her proposal wasn't simply about finding Cleopatra's tomb—it was about establishing something that had never existed before: the first Latin American archaeological mission in Egypt. The bureaucratic maze of Egyptian antiquities was notorious for crushing foreign ambitions. Countless well-funded European and American expeditions had been denied access to prime sites. Yet here was this Dominican woman, armed with her own money and an unshakeable conviction, asking for permission to dig where no one else saw promise.

What Martinez understood, and what others missed, was that Egypt needed fresh perspectives. The archaeological establishment had grown comfortable with conventional wisdom. They assumed that if Cleopatra's tomb existed at all, it would be found in Alexandria, buried beneath modern buildings or lost to the Mediterranean's depths. No one was seriously considering Taposiris Magna—a semi-ruined temple complex 30 miles west of Alexandria that most scholars dismissed as architecturally insignificant. The negotiations were grueling. Martinez remembers sitting in government offices, feeling the skeptical stares of officials who couldn't quite believe this foreign lawyer thought she could succeed where trained archaeologists had failed. But her research was meticulous. She had studied every ancient text, mapped every possible burial site, and applied the same forensic reasoning that had made her Dominican Republic's most feared criminal defense attorney.

When Egypt finally granted her the license—the first ever issued to a Latin American nation—Martinez felt the profound responsibility of representation. This wasn't just her excavation anymore. It belonged to every Dominican child who had ever been told their dreams were too big, every Latin American scholar who had been overlooked by European institutions, every woman who had been dismissed in a male-dominated field. The financial reality was stark. American and European universities offered substantial funding, complete with teams of graduate students and state-of-the-art equipment. Martinez turned them all down. She understood that accepting their money meant accepting their control, their methodology, their conclusions. If she was going to prove that Cleopatra lay beneath the sands of Taposiris Magna, she needed to do it under the Dominican flag.

The decision cost her personally. Martinez liquidated her law practice savings, sold property, and borrowed against her future to finance those first crucial seasons. Her husband watched nervously as their financial security evaporated into the desert heat. But Martinez had calculated something her critics missed: this wasn't just an archaeological gamble—it was an investment in history itself. By 2007, the Dominican-Egyptian mission had taken shape. Martinez established partnerships with Universidad Católica Santo Domingo, creating internship opportunities for Caribbean students who had never imagined studying pharaonic Egypt. The Dominican government, initially puzzled by their citizen's obsession with ancient queens, began to recognize the soft power potential of archaeological diplomacy.

The breakthrough came when Martinez secured her diplomatic appointment as Dominican Cultural Minister to Egypt. The position gave her official status, a diplomatic passport, and most importantly, legitimacy within Egypt's bureaucratic structure. She was no longer the eccentric foreign lawyer digging in the sand—she was a recognized cultural ambassador building bridges between two ancient civilizations.

Treasures from the Sand (2006-2020)

The first coin changed everything. In 2006, just months after beginning systematic excavation, Martinez's team unearthed a bronze coin bearing the unmistakable profile of Cleopatra VII. The image was clear, powerful—a queen staring directly at them across two millennia. Martinez held it in her palm and felt the electric connection between theory and evidence. What followed was a cascade of discoveries that revolutionized understanding of Taposiris Magna's importance. The site that other archaeologists had dismissed as an unfinished temple revealed itself as a complex ceremonial center with direct ties to Egypt's final dynasty. Foundation deposits confirmed that construction had occurred during the Ptolemaic period, exactly when Martinez's theories predicted.

The golden-tongued mummies, discovered in 2021, sent shockwaves through the archaeological community. These weren't ordinary burials—they were individuals prepared for direct communication with Osiris in the afterlife. The gold leaf amulets placed on their tongues represented the most expensive funerary practice available in ancient Egypt, reserved for people of extraordinary status or religious significance. Martinez's team methodically catalogued each discovery. The count steadily climbed: 100 artifacts, then 500, then 1,000. By 2018, they had uncovered more than 2,600 objects from a site where "everybody believed there was nothing to be found." The Cairo Museum's exhibition, "10 Years of Dominican Archaeology in Egypt," showcased 350 of the most significant pieces, marking the first Latin American contribution to Egyptology displayed in Egypt's premier institution.

The discoveries painted a vivid picture of daily life during Cleopatra's reign. Ceremonial pottery revealed religious practices, oil lamps illuminated domestic activities, and limestone vessels spoke to the site's role in storing precious commodities. Most significantly, the artifacts demonstrated continuous occupation during the precise period when Cleopatra would have been planning her final resistance against Rome. The sacred trench discovery in 2024 represented the mission's most dramatic breakthrough yet. Hidden near the temple wall, this deliberately concealed deposit contained over 330 coins, most bearing Cleopatra's image. These weren't random losses or offerings—they were systematically buried treasures, hidden with the kind of care reserved for religious relics or royal emergency funds.

Mixed with the coins, Martinez's team found items of startling intimacy: remnants of female makeup, models of unknown pharaohs, and a bronze ring dedicated to Hathor, goddess of love and beauty. Each artifact suggested preparation for a royal burial, as if someone had been gathering the personal effects needed to outfit a queen for eternity. The recognition came gradually, then all at once. International media began paying attention to the Dominican woman who was rewriting Egyptian archaeology. Academic conferences that had once ignored her theories now invited her as a keynote speaker. In 2025, Forbes recognized Martinez's achievements by including her on their prestigious "50 Over 50" global list, celebrating women who reach their peak performance after age 50.

But for Martinez, the external validation mattered less than the internal certainty she felt each time her team uncovered another piece of evidence. The desert was giving up its secrets, one artifact at a time, and each discovery reinforced her conviction that Cleopatra's story wasn't finished yet.

The Underwater Clue (2020-2024)

The tunnel changed the entire paradigm. In 2022, Martinez's ground-penetrating radar revealed a 4,300-foot passageway carved with mathematical precision, running directly from the temple toward the Mediterranean Sea. Egyptian officials called it a "geometric miracle"—perfectly straight, precisely angled, clearly the work of master engineers. When Martinez first descended into the tunnel, she felt the weight of anticipation pressing against her chest. The walls were smooth, carved from solid rock with the kind of attention to detail that suggested sacred purpose. But what struck her most powerfully was the tunnel's trajectory. It didn't curve or meander like most ancient passageways—it arrowed toward the sea with unmistakable intention.

The implications hit her like a revelation. For twenty years, she had been thinking terrestrially, assuming that Cleopatra's tomb lay somewhere beneath the temple complex. But what if the queen's final resting place wasn't under the sand at all? What if it lay beneath the waves?

Ancient Alexandria had been devastated by earthquakes and tsunamis in 365 CE. Entire sections of the royal quarter had disappeared beneath the Mediterranean, taking with them palaces, temples, and quite possibly, the most famous tomb in history. If Cleopatra had chosen Taposiris Magna as her burial site, and if that site had included maritime elements, then parts of the complex could now be underwater. The more Martinez studied ancient texts, the more this theory made sense. Cleopatra had been planning her death for months, possibly years. She knew that Octavian would search for her body, and would want to parade her corpse through Rome as the ultimate symbol of his victory. A hidden tomb, connected to a temple but protected by the sea, would have offered the security she needed.

The ceramic jars and pottery discovered within the flooded tunnel sections dated precisely to the Ptolemaic period. These weren't accidental artifacts—they were intentional deposits, placed there during the tunnel's active use. Martinez began to imagine ancient priests carrying sacred objects through this passageway, performing rituals that connected the temple's terrestrial power to the sea's eternal mystery. By 2024, the weight of evidence had convinced Martinez that her search needed to expand beyond archaeology into oceanography. She needed someone who understood the underwater world as intimately as she understood ancient Egypt. She needed someone who had proven that the impossible was merely difficult.

She needed Robert Ballard.

The decision to contact the Titanic discoverer felt both audacious and inevitable. Martinez had spent her career taking calculated risks, betting her reputation on theories that others dismissed. Reaching out to the world's most famous underwater explorer was simply the logical next step in her quest. When she composed that first email to Ballard's team, Martinez felt the familiar mixture of excitement and terror that had driven her throughout her Dominican legal career. She was proposing something unprecedented: a collaboration between terrestrial archaeology and deep-sea exploration, between ancient history and cutting-edge technology, between a criminal lawyer turned Egyptologist and an oceanographer who had redefined what was possible beneath the waves.

The desert had taught Martinez patience, persistence, and the value of following evidence wherever it led. Now the sea was calling, and she was ready to answer. Twenty years of systematic excavation had brought her to this moment—the recognition that Cleopatra's final secret might not be buried in sand at all, but resting in the blue depths of the Mediterranean, waiting for two worlds of exploration to finally come together.

The woman who had once promised her father she would find the truth about history's most famous queen was about to embark on the most ambitious phase of her quest. The desert had yielded its treasures, but the sea held the ultimate prize.

Chapter 6: The Historic Partnership Between Martinez and Ballard

The phone call that changed everything happened on an ordinary Tuesday morning in March 2024. Kathleen Martinez sat in her makeshift office at Taposiris Magna, surrounded by ceramic fragments and field notes, staring at her phone. For weeks, her team had been urging her to reach out to the world's most famous underwater explorer. "You're crazy if you think Bob Ballard will take your call," her assistant had warned. But Martinez had spent twenty years defying expectations, and she wasn't about to stop now.

The tunnel discovery had haunted her thoughts for months. Every night, she visualized that flooded passageway leading toward the Mediterranean, its ancient stones pointing like an arrow toward something magnificent hidden beneath the waves. Her land-based excavations had revealed tantalizing clues—hundreds of Cleopatra coins, golden-tongued mummies, sacred offerings buried in hidden trenches—but the tunnel whispered of secrets that lay beyond her reach. Martinez had always been methodical, approaching Cleopatra's mystery like the criminal cases that once made her reputation in Dominican courts. She analyzed evidence, followed leads, and never let emotional attachment cloud her judgment. But this felt different. The tunnel wasn't just another archaeological feature; it was a calling card from the past, demanding she venture into uncharted territory.

When she finally dialed Bob Ballard's number at the University of Rhode Island, her heart hammered against her ribs. The man who discovered the Titanic, who revolutionized deep-sea exploration, who commanded respect in scientific circles around the world—why would he care about her theory?

Ballard answered on the third ring, his voice carrying the casual confidence of someone accustomed to calls from around the globe. Martinez launched into her pitch, describing the tunnel system, the artifacts, and the growing evidence that Cleopatra's burial site extended into underwater chambers. She expected polite dismissal or requests for formal proposals.

Instead, Ballard's voice quickened with genuine excitement. "Tell me about these tunnels," he demanded. "How deep? What's the geological structure? Have you done any sonar mapping?"

The conversation stretched for ninety minutes. Ballard peppered Martinez with technical questions while she painted vivid descriptions of her discoveries. When she mentioned the sacred trench containing over 330 coins, all depicting Cleopatra's face, Ballard went silent for a full ten seconds.

"Kathleen," he finally said, "I've spent my career chasing shipwrecks and exploring the deep ocean. But the chance to help solve one of history's greatest mysteries? That's irresistible. When can I see this site?"

Within weeks, Ballard was boarding a plane to Egypt, accompanied by Dr. Larry Mayer, the renowned sonar expert from the University of New Hampshire's Center for Coastal and Ocean Mapping. Mayer brought decades of experience in advanced underwater acoustics, including pioneering work on 3-D seafloor visualization and Chirp Sonar technology. His participation elevated the expedition from ambitious theory to cutting-edge science. The Egyptian government, initially skeptical of expanding Martinez's excavation permits, recognized the prestige that Ballard's involvement would bring. The Ministry of Tourism and Antiquities fast-tracked approvals for underwater surveys, understanding that the collaboration between a Dominican archaeologist and America's most famous oceanographer would generate international attention for Egyptian archaeology.

Dr. Zahi Hawass, the legendary former director of Egypt's Supreme Council of Antiquities, had initially given Martinez just two months to prove her theories back in 2004. Now, twenty years later, he watched with fascination as she assembled what might become the most significant underwater archaeological expedition in Mediterranean history. The partnership defied conventional academic boundaries. Martinez brought an intuitive understanding of ancient burial practices and an unshakeable conviction about Cleopatra's final resting place. Ballard contributed technological expertise and the financial backing that comes with National Geographic sponsorship. Together, they represented a fusion of traditional archaeology with revolutionary exploration techniques.

But the collaboration faced skepticism from established Egyptologists who maintained that Cleopatra was buried somewhere in Alexandria's royal quarter, now lost beneath the harbor. Dr. Sarah Parcak, the space archaeologist known for satellite-based discoveries, publicly questioned whether resources should be diverted to underwater searches when so many terrestrial sites remained unexplored. Martinez felt the weight of academic disapproval but drew strength from Ballard's unwavering support. During their first meeting at Taposiris Magna, as she guided him through the temple complex and showed him the tunnel entrance, she watched his expression transform from professional curiosity to genuine wonder.

"Nobody's ever looked here before," he marveled, kneeling beside the flooded passageway. "In all my years exploring the Mediterranean, I never imagined finding Ptolemaic-era structures this far from shore."

Technology Meets Archaeology (2024)

The marriage of Martinez's archaeological intuition with Ballard's technological arsenal began in earnest during the summer of 2024. The team established a floating command center aboard the research vessel E/V Nautilus, equipped with the most sophisticated underwater exploration equipment available to civilian researchers. Ballard's approach to the Cleopatra mystery reflected lessons learned from decades of deep-sea exploration. Just as he had used advanced sonar to locate the Titanic in 1985, he now deployed next-generation acoustic mapping systems to peer beneath the Mediterranean seafloor. But this expedition presented unique challenges that shipwreck hunting never posed.

Ancient ports and temple complexes don't emit distinctive sonar signatures like steel hulls. Stone blocks weathered by millennia of saltwater corrosion blend into natural rock formations. Sediment accumulation can bury structures twenty feet deep, rendering them invisible to conventional survey techniques. The team needed to distinguish between natural geological features and human-made constructions that predated the Roman Empire. Dr. Larry Mayer's expertise proved invaluable in developing search protocols specifically adapted to archaeological targets. His team at the University of New Hampshire had pioneered multi-beam echo-sounding techniques that could map underwater topography with unprecedented precision. They modified their standard survey equipment to detect subtle anomalies that might indicate buried architecture.

The technological integration fascinated Martinez, who had spent two decades relying on traditional archaeological methods—careful excavation, artifact analysis, and historical research. Now she watched sonar operators identify potential dig sites from aboard a research vessel positioned miles offshore. Computer screens displayed three-dimensional models of underwater terrain, revealing hidden landscapes that no human eye had seen for centuries. Ballard's remotely operated vehicles (ROVs) represented the latest evolution in underwater exploration technology. Unlike the primitive black-and-white cameras that captured the first Titanic images in 1985, these modern systems transmitted high-definition color video through fiber-optic cables. Viewers on the surface could observe archaeological sites in real-time, directing exploration from comfortable command centers rather than descending in cramped submersibles.

The telepresence revolution that Ballard had championed throughout his later career brought Martinez's discoveries to global audiences instantaneously. Students in classrooms around the world could watch live as ROV cameras explored ancient structures. Interactive broadcasts allowed viewers to suggest search areas and ask questions of the archaeological team. Martinez initially felt overwhelmed by the technological complexity surrounding her straightforward mission: find Cleopatra's tomb. She was accustomed to quiet contemplation while examining pottery shards or carefully brushing sediment from buried coins. The expedition's command center buzzed with electronic activity—sonar operators calling out depth readings, video technicians adjusting camera angles, communications specialists coordinating with Egyptian Navy vessels.

But gradually, she began appreciating how technology amplified rather than replaced traditional archaeological skills. When ROV cameras revealed rectangular stone formations on the seafloor, her twenty years of experience studying Taposiris Magna's architecture allowed her to distinguish artificial constructions from natural rock outcrops.

The Egyptian Navy's participation added another layer of technological sophistication to the operation. Their vessels provided precise positioning data using military-grade GPS systems, ensuring that underwater discoveries could be accurately mapped relative to the temple complex onshore. Navy divers, trained in underwater archaeology protocols, could deploy to investigate targets identified through remote sensing. Ballard mapped approximately six miles of underwater terrain during the initial survey phase, creating a comprehensive baseline for future excavation planning. His team identified five primary areas of interest, each displaying characteristics suggesting human modification of the natural landscape.

The technological achievements impressed international observers, but Martinez remained focused on the fundamental archaeological question: did these underwater structures connect to Cleopatra's burial site? All the sophisticated equipment in the world couldn't substitute for the methodical analysis that archaeology demanded.

As she studied sonar images showing massive stone blocks arranged in systematic patterns, Martinez felt the same excitement that had driven her initial tunnel excavation. Technology was revealing possibilities that traditional archaeology could never access, but human interpretation would determine their significance.

The Five Search Sites (2024)

The underwater survey revealed a submerged landscape that defied every previous assumption about Taposiris Magna's ancient geography. What Martinez and Ballard discovered wasn't simply a flooded coastline; it was evidence of a sophisticated maritime complex that had supported major commercial and religious activities during Cleopatra's reign.

"Salam 5" emerged as the most intriguing target during the initial sonar sweeps. The name, chosen by Egyptian Navy personnel, reflected the site's peaceful appearance beneath the waves. But closer inspection revealed rectangular stone structures rising more than twenty feet from the seafloor, their geometric precision impossible to explain through natural geological processes. When ROV cameras first approached Salam 5, the images transmitted to the command center left both Martinez and Ballard speechless. Massive basalt pedestals, identical to broken statue foundations at the Taposiris Magna temple, stood in organized rows beneath forty feet of Mediterranean water. The structural similarity wasn't coincidental; these were clearly components of the same architectural complex.

Martinez studied the underwater formations with the same intensity she brought to every artifact discovery onshore. The pedestals' orientation aligned perfectly with the temple complex's sacred geometry, suggesting they once supported monuments or ceremonial installations. Their submersion resulted from the catastrophic earthquakes that repeatedly struck Egypt's northern coast between 320 and 1303 AD. The discovery validated Martinez's most audacious theory: Taposiris Magna hadn't simply been a religious site perched near the Mediterranean shore. It had been the terrestrial component of an integrated complex that extended far into what was now underwater territory. If Cleopatra's burial chamber lay within this expanded sacred precinct, traditional land-based searches might never locate it.

"Three Sisters" captured the team's attention during the second week of underwater surveys. Three stone pillars, each standing approximately fifteen feet tall, formed a triangular arrangement that maritime archaeologists immediately recognized as artificial. Natural rock formations don't create such geometric patterns, and the pillars' surface textures matched construction techniques documented at Ptolemaic-era sites throughout Egypt. Ballard's experience exploring ancient shipwrecks provided crucial context for interpreting the underwater structures. Mediterranean civilizations had routinely built harbors and ceremonial installations that extended below the high-tide line. What appeared unusual to land-based archaeologists represented standard ancient maritime architecture.

The pillars' positioning intrigued Martinez because they corresponded to astronomical alignments she had documented within the Taposiris Magna temple complex. Ancient Egyptian burial sites frequently incorporated celestial references, with architectural elements designed to guide the deceased's journey to the afterlife. If the Three Sisters served similar symbolic functions, they strengthened arguments for royal burial activities in the underwater zone. Additional anomalies scattered across the survey area provided supporting evidence for extensive ancient construction. Stone anchors of various sizes, some weighing several tons, indicated that the submerged port had accommodated large vessels. Amphora fragments dating to the Ptolemaic period confirmed commercial activity during Cleopatra's lifetime.

The discovery of a highly polished floor section beneath the sediment particularly excited Martinez. Ancient temples routinely featured elaborate paving designed to reflect torchlight during nighttime ceremonies. Finding similar architectural details in the underwater zone suggested that religious activities had extended beyond the terrestrial temple boundaries. Dr. Mayer's sonar mapping revealed the full scope of the submerged complex, tracing structural remains across nearly three square miles of seafloor. The underwater architecture displayed the same organizational principles that governed Taposiris Magna's design, with major features aligned along sacred axes that pointed toward celestial phenomena.

Ballard's geological analysis confirmed that the current coastline lay approximately 2.5 miles inland from its ancient position. Seismic activity over the centuries had dramatically altered the region's topography, submerging areas that once hosted major construction projects. The scale of geological change explained why previous archaeological expeditions had never suspected the existence of underwater components. For Martinez, the five search sites represented vindication of her twenty-year quest. Each discovery strengthened her conviction that Cleopatra's tomb lay within the expanded Taposiris Magna complex, possibly in chambers that were now accessible only through underwater approaches.

The National Geographic cameras captured every moment of revelation as Martinez and Ballard explored their underwater discoveries. When Martinez first observed the Salam 5 structures through ROV video feeds, tears streamed down her face. "After 2,000 years," she whispered, "nobody has ever been there. We are the first ones."

Ballard shared her emotional response, recognizing that this expedition might eclipse even his Titanic discovery in historical significance. Finding the world's most famous shipwreck had been a triumph of technology and persistence. But uncovering Cleopatra's final resting place would rewrite fundamental assumptions about ancient Egyptian civilization.

The collaboration had achieved its primary objective: expanding the search for Cleopatra's tomb beyond traditional boundaries. Whether the underwater structures would ultimately yield the queen's burial chamber remained unknown, but Martinez and Ballard had forever changed how archaeologists approached one of history's greatest mysteries.

Chapter 7: Descent Into History

The Mediterranean waters off Egypt's coast had never witnessed anything quite like this. In the summer of 2024, as the world grappled with global uncertainties, a different kind of drama was unfolding beneath the waves—one that would soon captivate millions of viewers and potentially rewrite ancient history.

When National Geographic executives first heard Kathleen Martinez's pitch about combining her two-decade land-based search with Bob Ballard's underwater expertise, they knew they were looking at something extraordinary. This wasn't just another archaeological documentary—this was the convergence of two legendary explorers at the height of their careers, pursuing history's most elusive prize. The investment was substantial. National Geographic committed to a full production crew, cutting-edge underwater filming technology, and months of on-location shooting across Egypt and the Mediterranean. Producer Sandra Maischberger, who had first interviewed Martinez years earlier, understood the emotional weight of what they were attempting to capture. "We weren't just documenting a search," she would later reflect. "We were potentially witnessing the moment when one of history's greatest mysteries gets solved." The pressure on Martinez was immense. After twenty years of promising discoveries that hadn't yet yielded Cleopatra's tomb, the cameras brought an uncomfortable reality: failure would now be broadcast to the world. During the documentary's Washington D.C. premiere in September 2025, Martinez admitted the emotional toll. "There were moments when I wondered if I was ready for the world to watch me succeed or fail on this scale. But then I remembered why I started this journey—for Cleopatra, for the Dominican Republic, and for every person who's been told their dreams are impossible." The filming process required delicate choreography. Archaeological excavation demands patience and precision, while television production operates on tight schedules and dramatic reveals. Director Andreas Veiel—fresh from his acclaimed work on controversial subjects—brought a different perspective to archaeological storytelling. Rather than sensationalizing the hunt, he focused on the human elements: Martinez's unwavering determination, Ballard's infectious enthusiasm, and the cultural significance of a Dominican woman potentially making the discovery of the century.

The international attention added layers of complexity Martinez hadn't anticipated. Egyptian government officials, initially supportive of the underwater expansion, became increasingly cautious as global media attention intensified. Every dive, every artifact, every theory required careful diplomatic navigation. The documentary crew captured these behind-the-scenes tensions, showing viewers the political realities that modern archaeologists face when working in foreign countries. Ballard found himself in an unfamiliar position. Unlike his previous deep-sea expeditions where he controlled most variables, this collaboration required adapting his methodical approach to Martinez's more intuitive style. The cameras captured their occasional disagreements—never heated, always respectful—about diving schedules, site prioritization, and interpretation of sonar readings. These moments revealed the genuine human dynamics behind their historic partnership.

The Underwater Discoveries (2024)

September 2024 marked a turning point that would define the entire documentary. As Ballard's team deployed their advanced sonar equipment in the Mediterranean waters adjacent to Taposiris Magna, the first images transmitted to their command center left everyone speechless.

"We started seeing structures," Ballard announced, his voice carrying the same excitement he'd felt when first glimpsing the Titanic's boilers. But these weren't the remains of a tragic shipwreck—these were deliberate constructions, arranged with purpose and built to last millennia. The underwater site revealed colossal constructions over twenty feet high, arranged in systematic rows that suggested careful urban planning. Polished floors, cemented blocks, and carefully positioned columns emerged from the sediment like ancient ghosts. Multiple anchors and amphora—the clay vessels used throughout the Greek and Roman worlds for transporting goods—littered the seafloor, creating an archaeological timeline that perfectly aligned with Cleopatra's reign.

Martinez floated on a raft above the dive site, radio crackling with updates from the underwater team. The documentary cameras captured her raw emotion as each discovery was reported. "This is one of those moments when you feel so alive," she said, tears mixing with Mediterranean spray. Her twenty-year theory was being validated in real-time, transmitted live to her floating command center. The structure dubbed "Salam 5" became the expedition's focal point. Several tall, flat rectangular stone formations rose from the seafloor, their design eerily reminiscent of the broken statue pedestals Martinez had discovered at the temple above. Nearby, divers located another formation they nicknamed the "Three Sisters"—three pillars standing sentinel in the underwater landscape, possibly marking significant boundaries or ceremonial spaces.

Ballard's excitement was palpable throughout the filming. "I have a very big smile on my face," he told Martinez over the radio. "There is an island with a harbor that has a tunnel leading from the temple, we think, to that very spot. This doesn't get any better." For a man who had discovered some of history's most famous underwater sites, his enthusiasm for Martinez's quest spoke volumes. The evidence suggested this wasn't just any ancient port—it was a sophisticated maritime infrastructure that had operated during Cleopatra's lifetime. Pottery shards recovered from the site dated precisely to the Ptolemaic period, while the amphora designs matched those used for transporting precious goods throughout the Mediterranean. The systematic arrangement of structures indicated this hadn't been a simple fishing village, but rather a major commercial and possibly ceremonial port.

Jonathan Fiely and Michael Barnette, Ballard's underwater archaeology specialists, worked methodically to map the site. Their detailed sonar readings revealed nearly six miles of underwater terrain, creating the most comprehensive map of the region's submerged landscape ever attempted. Each dive brought new revelations, each sonar pass revealed additional structures. The documentary captured the team's growing realization that they weren't just looking at an ancient port—they were potentially seeing the maritime infrastructure that had served Cleopatra's Egypt. Martinez's tunnel, discovered two years earlier and leading directly from the temple toward the sea, suddenly made perfect sense. This underwater port might have been where royal barges docked, where tribute from distant lands arrived, where the last pharaoh of Egypt conducted the business of her maritime empire.

The Sacred Trench Revelation (2024)

While cameras rolled underwater, equally dramatic discoveries were unfolding on land. Martinez's team, working just meters from where the documentary crew had set up their equipment, uncovered what would become one of the most significant archaeological finds of the 21st century. The "sacred trench," as Martinez termed it, lay hidden near the southern wall of the Taposiris Magna temple complex. For nearly two millennia, this carefully concealed cache had remained untouched, waiting for precisely the right moment to reveal its secrets. The timing felt almost supernatural—as if Cleopatra herself had orchestrated the discovery to coincide with the world's watching eyes.

Inside the trench, Martinez's team discovered 337 coins, most bearing the unmistakable profile of Cleopatra VII herself. These weren't casual losses or accidental deposits—they had been deliberately buried, carefully arranged, and ritually concealed. The coins' excellent preservation suggested they had been hidden quickly, possibly during the chaos following Cleopatra's death and the Roman conquest of Egypt. The documentary cameras captured Martinez's hands trembling as she held the first coins to emerge from the trench. Two decades of theoretical work suddenly became tangible reality. "This is clear evidence that Cleopatra was loved and they wanted to preserve things that were [from her time]," she explained to the camera. "They didn't want the Romans getting them."

Beyond the coins, the trench yielded an extraordinary collection of personal artifacts that seemed to tell the story of Egypt's last days of independence. Female makeup containers, still containing traces of ancient cosmetics, suggested the presence of royal women. A bronze ring dedicated to Hathor, goddess of love and beauty, bore a Greek inscription reading "the justice of Ra has arisen"—a phrase that resonated with both religious and political significance. Perhaps most intriguingly, the team discovered what appeared to be a marble bust of a woman wearing royal regalia. Martinez immediately recognized the significance—while other archaeologists would later debate whether the sculpture depicted Cleopatra or another Ptolemaic royal, its discovery in this sacred context suggested profound ritual importance. The bust's small size made it perfect for concealment, its white marble construction suggesting it had been crafted for someone of supreme importance.

The documentary captured the painstaking process of revealing each artifact. Unlike the dramatic excavation scenes often portrayed in Hollywood, real archaeology requires meticulous documentation, careful preservation, and exhaustive analysis. Every coin was photographed in situ before removal, every artifact carefully catalogued and preserved. The cameras showed viewers the unglamorous reality of archaeological work—hours of careful brushing, endless measurements, constant documentation. Dr. Zahi Hawass, Egypt's former Minister of Antiquities, appeared in the documentary to provide context for the discoveries. While he disputed some of Martinez's interpretations—particularly regarding the marble bust—he acknowledged the extraordinary nature of the find. "These artifacts represent the final moments of Ptolemaic Egypt," he observed. "Someone took great care to preserve these items from Roman destruction."

The trench also yielded oil lamps, ceremonial pottery, bronze statuettes, and a scarab amulet inscribed with religious texts. Each artifact added another piece to the puzzle Martinez had been assembling for twenty years. The collection painted a picture of deliberate preservation—not random burial, but careful ritual concealment designed to protect sacred objects from conquering forces. The timing of these land-based discoveries, coinciding perfectly with the underwater revelations, created a narrative arc that no scriptwriter could have improved. As Ballard's team mapped ancient maritime infrastructure offshore, Martinez's team was simultaneously uncovering evidence of the hurried efforts to preserve Egypt's royal legacy on land. The tunnel connecting these two sites suddenly took on profound significance—not just as an engineering marvel, but as a potential escape route, treasure pathway, or even a sacred corridor designed to connect the worlds of the living and the dead.

The documentary's final scenes captured Martinez standing at the entrance to her tunnel, Mediterranean waters visible in the distance where Ballard's team continued their underwater mapping. Twenty years of solitary work had evolved into international collaboration, theoretical archaeology had become tangible discovery, and a Dominican woman's childhood dream was reshaping our understanding of ancient Egypt. "For me, it's a matter of time," Martinez told the cameras in her final interview. "I'm not going to stop." The words carried weight earned through two decades of persistence, validation delivered through bronze coins and marble statues, and hope sustained by the knowledge that history's greatest mystery might finally be within reach.

As the documentary concluded, viewers worldwide understood they had witnessed more than just archaeological discovery. They had seen the power of unwavering determination, the beauty of international collaboration, and the profound moment when theoretical work transforms into historical revelation. Whether or not Cleopatra's tomb would ultimately be found, the journey itself had already made history.

Chapter 8: The Search Continues

The documentary cameras had captured their final shots, the diving equipment was carefully stored, and the research vessels had returned to port. But as September 2025 dawned, the story of Kathleen Martinez and Bob Ballard was just beginning its most thrilling chapter.

The September 2025 Breakthrough

When "Cleopatra's Final Secret" premiered on National Geographic on September 25, 2025, the world held its breath. The documentary didn't just tell a story—it revealed groundbreaking discoveries that sent shockwaves through the archaeological community and captured the imagination of millions. Martinez stood in her hotel room in Washington, D.C., where the documentary had premiered just hours earlier, watching her phone buzz with notifications from around the globe. Twenty years of dedication, countless setbacks, and moments of doubt had led to this moment. The underwater port discovery, documented in stunning detail by Ballard's advanced sonar systems, was no longer just a theory whispered in academic corridors—it was broadcast into living rooms worldwide.

The public reaction was immediate and overwhelming. Social media platforms exploded with discussions about the mysterious structures lying 20 feet beneath the Mediterranean waves. Amateur historians debated the significance of the 330 coins hidden in the sacred trench, while underwater photography enthusiasts marveled at the crystal-clear images of ancient amphora and stone anchors that hadn't been seen for two millennia. But perhaps most striking was how the collaboration between Martinez and Ballard had captured hearts. Here were two explorers from completely different worlds—a Dominican lawyer-turned-archaeologist and a Kansas-born ocean explorer—united by an impossible dream. Their partnership represented something larger than archaeological discovery; it embodied the power of international cooperation and the relentless human drive to uncover truth.

The international archaeological community's response was more complex. Oxford professor Andrew Meadows acknowledged the authenticity of the Cleopatra coins while maintaining skepticism: "Yes indeed, these are coins struck during the reign of Cleopatra, and bearing her portrait. Was she buried there? We have absolutely no ancient literary or documentary evidence to suggest so." Thomas Faucher from the Center for Alexandrian Studies echoed these doubts, noting that "the idea of Cleopatra [being] buried in Taposiris has long been rejected by a lot of scholars." Yet something had shifted in the academic discourse. The underwater discoveries added a new dimension that couldn't be easily dismissed. The tunnel leading from the temple directly to the submerged port suggested a sophisticated understanding of engineering and logistics that aligned perfectly with Martinez's theories about secret burial preparations. For the

Dominican Republic, Martinez's achievement represented a moment of profound national pride. President Luis Abinader issued a statement calling her work "a testament to Dominican ingenuity and perseverance on the world stage." Schools across the country organized viewing parties for the documentary, and young Dominican students began expressing interest in archaeology and marine science in unprecedented numbers. The ripple effects extended far beyond academic circles. Tourism inquiries to Egypt surged, with visitors specifically requesting tours of Taposiris Magna. The Egyptian Ministry of Tourism reported a 200% increase in archaeological tourism bookings within 48 hours of the documentary's premiere.

In the weeks following the documentary's success, Martinez and Ballard found themselves planning the most ambitious underwater archaeological expedition in modern history. The initial discoveries had raised more questions than answers, and both explorers knew they stood at the threshold of potentially revolutionary findings. The next phase would integrate cutting-edge technologies that didn't exist when Martinez began her quest in 2005. AI-powered underwater robotics were revolutionizing archaeological exploration, with machine learning algorithms capable of identifying specific features and objects on the ocean floor through advanced image and pattern recognition. These systems could process vast amounts of data in real-time, detecting anomalies and patterns that human eyes might miss.

Ballard's team was already developing specialized autonomous underwater vehicles (AUVs) designed specifically for archaeological work. Unlike traditional oceanographic robots built for geological surveys, these new machines carried delicate manipulation arms capable of carefully excavating artifacts without damage. The Stanford University-designed Ocean One, a humanoid robot capable of diving 2,000 meters, represented the next evolution in underwater archaeological tools. Martinez insisted on maintaining the Dominican identity of the project while embracing international collaboration. She established the Cleopatra Underwater Archaeological Institute in Santo Domingo, designed to train the next generation of diving archaeologists from across Latin America. The institute's first class of 20 students included marine biologists, classical archaeologists, and underwater photographers from Mexico, Colombia, Brazil, and Peru.

The training program was revolutionary in its scope. Students learned not just traditional archaeological methods, but also underwater robotics operation, AI-assisted data analysis, and advanced diving techniques for working at depths up to 100 meters. Martinez had dreamed of this moment—creating opportunities for Latin American scientists to participate in groundbreaking research that would have global impact. Ballard, meanwhile, was developing what he called "telepresence archaeology"—using real-time video feeds and robotic manipulation to allow archaeologists on the surface to conduct precise excavations hundreds of feet underwater. The technology could potentially allow Martinez to direct excavations from her research station while doctoral students in universities around the world watched and learned in real-time.

The preservation challenges were enormous. Artifacts that had been protected by sediment and seawater for 2,000 years would require immediate conservation once exposed. The team was collaborating with conservation laboratories in Egypt, the United States, and the Dominican Republic to ensure that any discoveries could be properly preserved for future study. Funding came from an unexpected consortium of sources. National Geographic committed to a multi-year documentary series. The Dominican government allocated emergency research funds. The Egyptian Ministry of Tourism invested in infrastructure improvements around Taposiris Magna. Even private foundations focused on women in science contributed significant grants, inspired by Martinez's groundbreaking achievement.

Legacy of the Collaboration

The partnership between Martinez and Ballard had created something unprecedented in modern archaeology—a truly collaborative model that bridged traditional land-based excavation with advanced underwater exploration. Their success was already inspiring similar collaborations worldwide. In Greece, marine archaeologists were partnering with the team that discovered the Antikythera wreck to search for additional ancient vessels using Ballard-inspired techniques. Off the coast of Turkey, researchers were applying Martinez's theoretical framework to investigate underwater Byzantine ruins. The methodological innovations from the Cleopatra project were spreading throughout the field.

Martinez's role in inspiring Latin American scientists was perhaps the most personally meaningful aspect of her achievement. Universities across the region were establishing new marine archaeology programs, and young women were enrolling in unprecedented numbers. The Martinez Fellowship, funded by a consortium of Dominican businesses, was providing full scholarships for promising students to pursue advanced degrees in underwater archaeology..Ballard, at 83, found renewed energy in the collaboration. The Titanic discovery had made him famous, but working with Martinez had reminded him why he became an ocean explorer in the first place—the pure joy of discovery and the responsibility to share that excitement with the world. His lectures now frequently featured stories from the Cleopatra expedition, emphasizing how international collaboration could achieve what no single researcher could accomplish alone.

The technological innovations were having impacts far beyond archaeology. The AI systems developed for identifying ancient artifacts were being adapted for environmental monitoring, helping marine biologists track coral reef health and identify invasive species. The University of Minnesota's MeCO project was already using similar AI-powered underwater robots to identify and track invasive species in lakes..The economic impact was substantial. Egypt was experiencing a renaissance in archaeological tourism. The Dominican Republic was attracting international research partnerships that brought both prestige and economic benefits. Equipment manufacturers were developing new products specifically for underwater archaeology, creating jobs and spurring innovation in marine technology. But perhaps most importantly, the collaboration had demonstrated that archaeology was not just about the past—it was about building bridges between cultures, generations, and disciplines. Martinez and Ballard had shown that a criminal lawyer from Santo Domingo and an oceanographer from Kansas could find common ground in the depths of the Mediterranean Sea.

As 2025 drew to a close, the ultimate question remained unanswered: Would Cleopatra's tomb finally be found?

Martinez remained optimistic, even as she acknowledged the challenges ahead. "We will continue searching on land and underwater," she declared, adding that she felt finding Cleopatra's tomb was "a matter of time." The underwater port discovery had fundamentally changed the search parameters. If Cleopatra had indeed been secretly transported to Taposiris Magna through underwater channels, the tomb could be in areas that had never been systematically explored. The discoveries already made were reshaping understanding of ancient Egypt in ways that extended far beyond the search for one specific tomb. The evidence suggested that Taposiris Magna was not just a religious site but a sophisticated maritime complex with infrastructure that could support clandestine operations. This painted a picture of the final days of Ptolemaic Egypt that was more complex and dramatic than previously imagined.

Ballard approached the question with the systematic optimism of a veteran explorer. He had spent decades searching for seemingly impossible targets in the vast ocean. The Titanic had taken multiple attempts and years of preparation. The Bismarck required cutting-edge technology and innovative search strategies. Each discovery had seemed impossible until it wasn't.

The collaboration had already achieved something remarkable—it had brought two different worlds of exploration together in ways that would outlast any single discovery. Whether or not they found Cleopatra's tomb, Martinez and Ballard had created a new model for international archaeological cooperation that would influence research for generations. For Martinez, the search represented something deeper than professional achievement. It was about proving that dreams deferred need not be dreams denied. At 59, she had spent more than a third of her life pursuing this goal. The young girl who had argued with her father about Cleopatra's true character had become the world's leading expert on the queen's final days.

The enduring mystery continued to captivate the world because it represented fundamental human questions about love, power, death, and legacy. Cleopatra VII had been one of history's most powerful women, a brilliant politician and strategist who had nearly changed the course of the Roman Empire. Her relationship with Julius Caesar and Mark Antony had shaped the ancient world. Her final choice to die by suicide rather than submit to Roman humiliation had become the stuff of legend. But beyond the historical significance was the simple human desire to solve a puzzle that had confounded scholars for over 2,000 years. In an age of satellite mapping and deep-sea exploration, the fact that such a significant historical figure's burial place remained unknown seemed almost impossible. Yet that impossibility was precisely what made the search so compelling.

As Martinez and Ballard prepared for the next phase of their expedition, they carried with them not just advanced technology and decades of experience, but the hopes and curiosity of millions of people around the world. They had become the public face of a quest that belonged to all of humanity—the drive to understand our past and the courage to pursue seemingly impossible dreams. The search for Cleopatra's tomb had brought together a Dominican lawyer and a Kansas oceanographer in the depths of the Mediterranean Sea. In doing so, it has proven that the most extraordinary discoveries often come from the most unexpected partnerships. Whether they ultimately found the queen's final resting place or not, Martinez and Ballard had already uncovered something equally valuable—the power of collaboration, persistence, and the refusal to accept that some mysteries are meant to remain unsolved forever.

Their story was far from over. In the depths of the Mediterranean, ancient secrets still waited to be revealed. And somewhere in those underwater chambers and submerged passages, the truth about history's most famous queen might finally surface, brought to light by two explorers who had dared to believe that the impossible was simply another word for not yet accomplished.

The Courage To Dream The Impossible

Standing at the edge of the Mediterranean Sea in September 2025, watching divers emerge from waters that hadn't been explored for two thousand years, Kathleen Martinez finally allowed herself a moment to breathe. Twenty-one years after first setting foot in Egypt with nothing but a theory and stubborn determination, she could see the culmination of what many had called impossible. The collaboration with Bob Ballard hadn't just brought advanced technology to her search—it had validated everything she'd sacrificed for.

The numbers tell one story: over 2,600 artifacts discovered, more than 300 coins bearing Cleopatra's image, and now an ancient underwater port that connects directly to the temple through a 4,300-foot tunnel. But the real story lives in the spaces between those statistics, in the moments when dreams refuse to die despite every rational reason to abandon them. Martinez's journey began with a young lawyer's argument with her father about a queen's true character. It evolved into something far more profound—a testament to what happens when someone refuses to accept the limitations others place on their vision. Her insistence on maintaining the Dominican identity of the project, repeatedly rejecting funding from American and European universities, wasn't just about national pride. It was about proving that breakthrough discoveries don't require traditional pathways or established institutional backing.

The moment Ballard agreed to join her expedition represented more than just a meeting of expertise—it symbolized the convergence of two different ways of dreaming the impossible. At 83, Ballard continues exploring the ocean, returning in July 2025 from a 21-day expedition mapping World War II battle sites in the Solomon Islands. His philosophy remains unchanged: "I like it when kids tell me to stop discovering something—it means there's still something to search for in the world." This partnership challenges our assumptions about how great discoveries happen. We expect breakthrough moments to emerge from well-funded laboratories or prestigious universities. Instead, the search for Cleopatra's tomb has been driven by a Dominican lawyer who taught herself archaeology and an American oceanographer who still gets excited about what lies beneath the next wave. Their collaboration proves that revolutionary discoveries often come from combining different forms of expertise, different ways of seeing the same problem.

The emotional weight of their work extends far beyond archaeology. Martinez sees Cleopatra as more than a historical figure: "She was a philosopher. She was a doctor in medicine. She was a chemist. She was a specialist in cosmetology." Her determination to find the queen's tomb represents a larger effort to rescue a brilliant woman's legacy from centuries of Roman propaganda and male-dominated historical narratives. Watching the underwater footage from the recently discovered port, you can hear the excitement in Ballard's voice as he tells Martinez over satellite phone: "There is an island with a harbor that has a tunnel leading from the temple, we think, to that very spot. This doesn't get any better." His enthusiasm reflects something deeper than professional satisfaction—it's the joy of someone who has spent his life pushing boundaries discovering that there are still new frontiers to explore.

The technical achievements of their collaboration represent a quantum leap in underwater archaeology. Ballard's telepresence technology allows scientists ashore to participate in real-time exploration, fundamentally changing how discoveries are made and shared. But the human element remains paramount. When Martinez stands in that ancient tunnel, knowing she's walking where Cleopatra's funeral procession might have passed, the moment transcends technology.

Their work has already changed how we understand the ancient world. The discovery of the underwater port proves that Taposiris Magna was far more than a religious site—it was a major maritime trading hub, suggesting the temple complex played a crucial role in Cleopatra's final days. Whether or not the tomb lies beneath those Mediterranean waters, the partnership has revolutionized our understanding of how ancient Egypt operated. The broader implications of their collaboration extend into education and inspiration. Martinez has become a role model for Latin American scientists, proving that breakthrough research doesn't require following traditional academic paths. Ballard's decades-long commitment to educational outreach, including his work with the Corps of Exploration and the Ocean Exploration Trust, continues inspiring new generations to pursue careers in science and exploration.

Perhaps most importantly, their story demonstrates the power of refusing to accept conventional wisdom. When Martinez first proposed that Cleopatra wasn't buried in Alexandria, established Egyptologists dismissed her theory. Zahi Hawass, Egypt's former antiquities chief, publicly stated that "the Egyptians never buried inside a temple" and declared her hypothesis unlikely. Today, with mounting archaeological evidence supporting her theory, those same experts are forced to reconsider assumptions that had stood unchallenged for decades. The collaboration also highlights how different forms of expertise can complement each other in unexpected ways. Martinez's legal training taught her to treat Cleopatra's case like a criminal investigation, following evidence wherever it led. Ballard's engineering background enabled him to develop the technological tools needed to explore previously inaccessible underwater sites. Neither could have achieved these discoveries alone.

Their partnership represents hope for the future of scientific exploration. In an era when funding often goes to safe, incremental research, Martinez and Ballard have shown that the biggest discoveries come from taking significant risks. Their willingness to bet their reputations on theories others considered impossible demonstrates the courage required for genuine breakthrough discoveries.

As Martinez stated recently, "Nobody can tell me that Cleopatra is not at Taposiris Magna. To say that you have to excavate the whole area and not find her." Her unwavering confidence, backed now by substantial archaeological evidence and advanced underwater exploration technology, embodies the kind of determination that drives human progress. The story of Cleopatra's Final Secret isn't really about finding an ancient tomb. It's about what becomes possible when someone with enough courage decides to dream the impossible, and then finds another dreamer willing to help make it reality. Their collaboration proves that the most important discoveries happen not when we follow established pathways, but when we have the audacity to create entirely new ones.

Standing together at the edge of discovery, Martinez and Ballard represent something timeless about human exploration. They remind us that beneath the Mediterranean waves, beneath the sands of Egypt, beneath everything we think we know about the world, extraordinary mysteries still wait for people brave enough to search for them. Their story challenges each of us to ask: What impossible dream are we allowing others to convince us to abandon? What discovery might be waiting for the person bold enough to believe it's possible? In the end, regardless of what lies buried beneath Taposiris Magna, Martinez and Ballard have already achieved something remarkable. They've shown us that the courage to dream the impossible isn't just about finding ancient treasures—it's about discovering what becomes possible when we refuse to accept the limitations others place on our vision. Their collaboration stands as proof that the greatest adventures in human history have always begun with someone willing to believe that impossible just means no one has tried hard enough yet.

Printed in Poland
by Amazon Fulfillment
Poland Sp. z o.o., Wrocław
26 January 2026

c9e2b60a-75f7-4d08-b674-68e244a9438cR01